THE CASE FOR
BAHÁ'U'LLÁH

THE CASE FOR BAHÁ'U'LLÁH

*A Journalist Examines
the Bahá'í Faith's Central Claim*

by Gary L. Matthews

Stonehaven Press
3101 Woodbine Avenue
Knoxville, Tennessee 37914

STONEHAVEN PRESS
3101 Woodbine Avenue
Knoxville, Tennessee 37914

e-mail: info@stonehaven-press.com
web: http://www.stonehaven-press.com

ISBN 978-1-893124-09-7

This book is an abridgement of *The Challenge of Bahá'u'lláh*
by Gary L. Matthews. Portions reproduced and adapted
under license from George Ronald, Publisher,
46 High Street, Oxford OX5 2DN, England

Cover design by
Cheri Matthews
Cover photo of Bryce Canyon
Copyright © Kwiktor / Dreamstime.com
http://www.dreamstime.com/bryce-canyon-image20496265

The Case for Bahá'u'lláh is
dedicated to the loving memory of
ROBERT L. GULICK JR. AND BAHIA GULICK

By the same author

CONTENTS

Abbreviations

The following abbreviations are used in the text. Please refer to the Bibliography for full details.

AB	'Abdu'l-Bahá (Balyuzi)	PHW	Persian Hidden Words
ADJ	The Advent of Divine Justice	PM	Prayers and Meditations
		PT	Paris Talks
AHW	Arabic Hidden Words	PUP	The Promulgation of Universal Peace
BNE	Bahá'u'lláh and the New Era		
		Q	The Qur'án
BWF	Bahá'í World Faith	RSV	Revised Standard Version Bible
CF	Citadel of Faith		
DB	The Dawn-Breakers	SAQ	Some Answered Questions
ESW	Epistle to the Son of the Wolf		
		SDC	The Secret of Divine Civilization
G	Gleanings from the Writings of Bahá'u'lláh		
		SWA	Selections from the Writings of 'Abdu'l-Bahá
GPB	God Passes By		
KI	Kitáb-i-Íqán (Book of Certitude)	SWB	Selections from the Writings of the Báb
		TAB	Tablets of 'Abdu'l-Bahá
LG	Lights of Guidance	TB	Tablets of Bahá'u'lláh
MA	Messages to the Antipodes	UD	The Unfolding Destiny of the British Bahá'í Community
NEB	New English Bible		
NIV	New International Version Bible		
		WOB	The World Order of Bahá'u'lláh.
PB	The Proclamation of Bahá'u'lláh		
PDC	The Promised Day is Come		

CASE NOTES

THE CASE FOR BAHÁ'U'LLÁH is not primarily about "what Bahá'ís believe". It is a book about *why* Bahá'ís believe as we do – or why, at any rate, this Bahá'í believes as he does. It shares my admittedly personal understanding of why it makes sense, and feels right, to accept the authority of Bahá'u'lláh as God's Messenger for this age.

In setting forth these grounds, I hope to reach the widest possible audience. This means doing two things:

First, it means critiquing Bahá'u'lláh's claim from the standpoint of logic and common sense. There already are many publications seeking to demonstrate His authenticity by interpreting symbolic Bible prophecies fulfilled in His advent. This book, however, refrains from assuming the reader to be of any particular religious belief. The only appeal here is to universal "first principles" – premises I find both logically and intuitively compelling, and which I dare hope may prove similarly satisfying to others.

Second, it means utilizing fully the tools of my trade as a journalist. I am not a historian, a scientist, a theologian, or an academic specialist in any technical field. It is my job to learn from such experts, to ask them probing questions, and to translate their answers into plain speech for "the rest of us". My college degree in English reinforces a lifelong love affair with language; my degree in journalism helps me to use that love as a tool for learning and communication. For several years after college, I worked as a reporter for a regional newspaper chain, then later as editor of a weekly newspaper (both in Middle Tennessee). There I covered all the usual beats – government, education, court battles, police work and the like. My favorite activity, bar none, was science reporting. The nearness of several large research facilities (such as the University of Tennessee Space Institute in Tullahoma) gave me ample scope to indulge this passion.

Since then I have also worked in printing and graphic design, and now, for nearly two decades, as publisher and principal writer for Stonehaven Press (the company founded by my wife Cheri and me). Whatever the outward details, I think of myself, first and foremost, as a journalist; and it is in that spirit that I write.

That spirit greatly affects the way I view the Bahá'í Faith. Although I am a second-generation Bahá'í, my spiritual life has hardly been smooth sailing. My journalistic training and temperament impel me to ask tough questions even about my own most cherished beliefs – especially, in fact, about those. Bahá'u'lláh claims not only to be God's latest Messenger but the Promised One of all ages and religions. This is a challenging proposition, certainly not one to be accepted lightly or blindly. How (I always wondered) might an honest investigator evaluate objectively its merits? More personally, how might I myself do so? Bahá'u'lláh asks no one to accept Him on mere faith: He advises every seeker to "examine His clear evidence" to "ascertain whether or not such a light hath appeared" (G 45, 103).

Given this mandate, I felt confirmed in searching, as a journalist, for every last scrap of evidence that might shed light on the truth or falsity of Bahá'u'lláh's claim. More often than not, that search entailed digging for clues that might disprove His assertions. I collected, and closely examined, any and all facts that might potentially refute, undermine, or discredit Bahá'u'lláh's authenticity. Why? Because in science, it is usually far easier to disprove a hypothesis than to validate it. Good scientists therefore proceed by striving to punch holes in their own favorite theories. Only those ideas that survive all the most rigorous, wrenching tests eventually may be accepted as provisionally true (subject always to further testing). This strikes me as one reasonable way to approach Bahá'u'lláh and the Bahá'í Faith.

My investigation spanned 35 years, during which my findings arranged themselves into a striking and in many ways surprising pattern. This book is a record of those findings and of the conclusions I drew from them.

*****

It is not, however, the first or only such record. As stated on its copyright page, *The Case for Bahá'u'lláh* is a condensed version of an earlier, considerably larger book of mine titled *The Challenge of Bahá'u'lláh*. The latter work has so far seen three editions (1993, 1999, and 2005). The first two were from George Ronald, Publisher (Oxford, England). The third was from Bahá'í Publishing (Wilmette, Illinois, USA) under license from George Ronald, whose management also graciously authorized this Stonehaven Press abridgment you are reading.

The original book (*Challenge*) distills decades of research and reflection into a space I consider fairly tight, given the amount of ground it covers. It was not easy to further boil down that much material into this even smaller package. At times I despaired of ever doing so. One saving grace was the emergence of the Internet as a reference tool. In *Challenge*, many crucial arguments hinge on historical or scientific facts that once were little known and hard to find. These required painstaking documentation and, at times, lengthy explanation. Today most of that same information lies at the fingertips of anyone with access to a good search engine. (As noted in the bibliography, for example, various books that were long out of print during my original research are today available online through the amazing Google Books project.) This makes it practical for a summary overview such as this to skim lightly over secondary details, focusing instead on the big picture and its underlying logic.

But why publish an abridged version at all? No digest can ever supplant its parent volume. Of my several books, *Challenge* remains my favorite. The investigation it describes represents, in some ways, my spiritual autobiography, my will and testament. But time has convinced me of the growing need for a synopsis such as *The Case for Bahá'u'lláh*. Today we all are pressed for time and drowning in information. All of us, up to and including heads of state, get most of our news not from newspapers but from news summaries. We then use these to determine which stories warrant a closer look. The art of summarizing has always been an integral part of journalism, but never more so than now.

I hope this volume, brief as it is, will encourage its readers to take a closer look at the amazing evidence that supports Bahá'u'lláh's claim. Every seeker will find a wealth of resources (including, of course, *The Challenge of Bahá'u'lláh* itself). Whenever any book of mine opens at least as many questions as it answers, then – and only then – do I feel validated as a reporter.

*****

Without legions of wonderful helpers, this book could never have seen daylight. Foremost among these is my wife and best friend, Cheri Wallace Matthews. The life of a writer is seldom easy, but it is far, far easier than living with one! Always my most helpful critic, Cheri cautions me when I am too brash, urges me on when I am too cautious, and pins me down when I am too vague or obscure. In this case, she also designed the exquisite cover (as she does for most Stonehaven books).

Another particularly central collaborator was the late Marzieh Gail, whose loving spirit lights these pages. Herself an outstanding journalist, it was she who first encouraged me, while I was a student, to pursue a career in that field. She it was also who set me on many of the trails explored in *Challenge* (and this book), and who, through steady correspondence, helped sort out clues and questions that cropped up along the way. When *Challenge* was complete, she was kind enough to give it a thorough polishing. This was among the last acts of her remarkable life, the earthly phase of which ended in October 1993.

This book would not exist without feedback from the many readers of *Challenge* who assured me that the information it contains helped them just as it has helped me.

Of course, everyone who assisted in the writing and publication of that original volume also contributed, directly and indirectly, to this one. Though too numerous to list, these individuals include Sam McClellan, Vahid Alavian, Charles Coffey, Kenneth Kalantar, Joel Brunson, the Research Department of the Universal House of Justice, and the National Spiritual Assembly of the Bahá'ís of Grenada, West Indies.

Far from least are the wonderful folks associated with George Ronald, Publisher, in Oxford – notably May Ballerio, Wendi Momen, and Erica Leith.

To Wendi Momen I am grateful for teaching me the system of abbreviated inline references I have borrowed in this volume to document citations. (These replace the section of endnotes used in all three editions of *The Challenge of Bahá'u'lláh*.) This system mimics, in some ways, the notation style endorsed by the Modern Language Association. I have, however, freely modified it to better reflect the material referenced herein.

Whenever I have felt it necessary to clarify terms used in quotations from other writers, I have used [brackets] to identify my insertions. Unless specified otherwise, however, all instances of *italics* or (parentheses) in quotations are those of the writer being quoted.

INTRODUCTION

RELIGION IS A SYSTEM OF BELIEF, but it is also much more: It is voluntary submission to a Higher Power. This remains true whether we interpret that power as a living God, an impersonal cosmic force, or simply some noble purpose. Religion means joyous surrender, a giving of ourselves to something greater than ourselves.

No one was ever argued into such a commitment any more than anyone was ever argued into falling in love. It is not enough for religion to make sense intellectually; it must also feel right and ring true in the very depth of one's being. Beyond that, it requires deliberate choice, an act of courage and humility that must spring as much from the heart as from the head. Sometimes linear thought plays only a minor role: Persons with sharp insight may embrace a religion – knowing exactly why they choose to do so – long before they can explain or justify the logic of their decision to anyone else. Instinctively, they simply know.

Just the same, we can recognize these facts and still agree with Bertrand Russell: "What is wanted is not the will to believe, but the wish to find out, which is the exact opposite." There is deep satisfaction in thinking clearly and rationally about religion and exchanging ideas with other people. Without the illumination of spiritual intuition, reason is sterile; but without the discipline of reason, intuition can be hard to distinguish from blind emotionalism – or, worse yet, from blind imitation.

The sacred writings of the Bahá'í Faith clearly define the role of reason in attaining spiritual insight. These teachings advise a seeker to

"apply thyself to rational and authoritative arguments. For arguments are a guide to the path and by this the heart will be turned unto the Sun of Truth. And when the heart is turned unto the Sun, then the eye will be opened and will recognize the Sun through the Sun itself. Then man will be in no need of arguments. . . ." (BWF 383-4)

"In divine questions we must not depend entirely upon the heritage of tradition and former human experience; nay, rather, we must exercise reason, analyze and logically examine the facts presented so that confidence will be inspired and faith attained." (PUP 327)

13

This book is the fruit of one person's struggle to understand and fulfill these admonitions. It seeks to present, in rational terms, the basis for my belief that the Bahá'í revelation is divine in origin, and to explain why I see its claim as posing a challenge of critical importance to humanity. Since religious conviction has roots that go far deeper than words or logic, it would be presumptuous to call this book a complete statement of my reasons for being a Bahá'í. Those reasons that I can explain in print constitute only one aspect (and not necessarily the most important aspect) of the experiences and promptings that have helped shape my belief. Nevertheless, I share them in the hope that they will prove useful or stimulating.

This book is primarily for two large groups of people: (1) those interested in the Bahá'í Faith but not committed to it; and (2) those already committed to the Faith who want to know more about the evidence upon which its claims rest. However, some readers may be hearing of the Bahá'í Faith for the first time. For them I have tried to provide, as the discussion unfolds, whatever background information is needed for an understanding of the points raised.

Chapter One
A TURNING POINT IN HISTORY

The major advances in civilization are processes which all but wreck the societies in which they occur.
—Alfred North Whitehead

... we must rise above the storm, the chaos of surface detail, and from a higher vantage-point look for the outline of some great and significant phenomenon. To rise up so as to see clearly is what I have tried to do, and it has led me to accept, however improbable they may appear, the reality and the consequences of the major cosmic process which ... I have called "human planetization."
—Pierre Teilhard de Chardin

HUMANITY CLEARLY IS passing through a crisis of transition. But a transition to what? It is easy to see turbulent changes wherever we look; easier still to see we all have a stake in those changes. It is not so easy to see what they mean, where they are taking us, or how we can respond constructively. Millions of people, sensing the importance of such questions, are earnestly seeking answers.

I believe those answers will elude us until we come to grips with an issue the world has evaded for more than a century:

Who was Bahá'u'lláh?

It may sound unlikely that the identity of this Persian nobleman who lived from 1817 to 1892 can shed any light on the upheavals that fill modern headlines. A "Who's Who"-style biographical sketch would tell us little – merely that He founded the Bahá'í Faith and spent forty years in prison and exile for proclaiming a message of peace and love. Marginally useful information, perhaps, in studying for a trivia quiz; but hardly crucial to an understanding of current events.

This being so, we must clarify the deeper sense in which it is important to ask who Bahá'u'lláh really was. First, however, some historical observations may make it easier to see the modern relevance of this question.

It is an intriguing fact that each major world religion – Hinduism, Judaism, Zoroastrianism, Buddhism, Christianity, and Islam – has given birth to a great civilization. These historic civilizations all have certain things in common. Each, in its turn, became the highest and most advanced culture the world had known until that time. Each, at its height, absorbed and unified hundreds of warring ethnic groups into a spiritual brotherhood. Each later declined and decayed to become more a source of conflict than of cooperation.

This cyclic rise and fall of civilizations – deriving their initial impulse from religion – has largely shaped the modern world. For example, the Hebrew culture derived from Judaism fertilized the philosophy of ancient Greece and left a code of law that became the basis for every modern legal system. When the Roman Empire collapsed, Christianity rose from its rubble, founded the new world of the West, and institutionalized a spirit of charity and philanthropy that still survives. As Western Europe sank into the Dark Ages, Islam molded primitive Arab tribes into an empire more vast than that of Rome at its peak, adorned its cities with flourishing universities and libraries, invented soap, algebra, Arabic numerals, and hundreds of other modern conveniences, and (during its centuries in Spain) indirectly triggered Europe's Renaissance. Moreover, it was Islam that introduced nationalism in the modern sense – a concept that, whatever its limitations, has spurred social and economic development throughout the world. Similar comments could be made about the magnificent civilizations engendered by Hinduism, Buddhism, and Zoroastrianism.

Each of these religious systems arose from the teachings of a single remarkable individual. Thus Moses became the central figure of Judaism, Jesus of Christianity, Muḥammad of Islam, Krishna of Hinduism, Buddha of Buddhism, and Zoroaster of Zoroastrianism. These spiritual guides are easily the most influential figures in history, for it is they who shaped and inspired the civilizations that followed them. Their lives and teachings exhibit uncanny similarities. Each claimed to derive His influence and authority directly from God. Each was known for saintly character and vast intuitive knowledge. Each was bitterly opposed by the civil and religious authorities of His time. Each attracted a small community of followers who (often after centuries of struggle) triumphed over persecution to establish the given faith as a major force in society. Each taught the same basic spiritual concepts regarding belief in God, life after death, prayer, self-discipline, ethical principles such as the Golden Rule, and the like. Each, however, modified the previous religion's social laws and regulations according to the needs of the changed time. Each reaffirmed the divine origin of previous religions, and each promised that God would send future messengers with new and fuller revelations.

The most remarkable parallel among these religions is found in their prophecies concerning the "last days." Each faith anticipates a culmination of human history when the earth, as a result of fiery tribulations, will be transformed into paradise. Cataclysmic changes will produce the "Kingdom of God on earth" (Matt. 6:10) in which the nations "shall beat their swords into plowshares, and their spears into pruninghooks: nation shall not lift up sword against nation, neither shall they learn war any more." (Isa. 2:4) The various religions will be gathered under "one fold and one shepherd" (John 10:16) and "the earth shall be full of the knowledge of the Lord, as the waters cover the sea." (Isa. 11:9) Substantially identical prophecies abound not only in the Old and New Testaments but also in the scriptures of all the world's historic faiths.

These same prophecies, with one voice, foretell the appearance of a World Reformer or Divine Teacher destined to initiate the promised changes. The central hope of every world faith revolves around the coming of such a spiritual leader, often identified as the "return" of the founder of the religion embodying the prophecy. In Judaism this Promised One is known as the Lord of Hosts; in Christianity, as the Second Coming of Christ; in Islam, as the Mihdí or Twelfth Imám; in Hinduism, as the return of Krishna; in Buddhism, as the Fifth Buddha; and in Zoroastrianism, as the promised Sháh-Bahrám.

Simply stated, the histories, teachings, and prophecies of these religions offer parallels far too numerous and too remarkable to be explained as mere coincidence. How can this seemingly arbitrary pattern repeat itself, age after age, in movements so widely separated by time, geography, and culture? Does this not suggest the possibility that all of them (not merely one or two) are truly divine in origin, that their founders were each inspired by a merciful God as agents of one vast civilizing process guiding humanity towards maturity? Would it not follow that their latter-day prophecies, foreshadowing the radical transformation of society through the influence of a promised redeemer, all point to the same mysterious Figure?

Bahá'ís believe that such is indeed the case. The hallmark of their faith is acceptance of Bahá'u'lláh's claim that He Himself is the Promised One of *all* religions – the long-awaited Peace-bringer Whose revelation, as foretold in earlier scriptures, will bring into being a worldwide divine civilization. He states:

> *"The Revelation which, from time immemorial, hath been acclaimed as the Purpose and Promise of all the Prophets of God, and the most cherished Desire of His Messengers, hath now . . . been revealed unto*

17

men. The advent of such a Revelation hath been heralded in all the sacred Scriptures. Behold how, notwithstanding such an announcement, mankind hath strayed from its path and shut out itself from its glory." (G 5)

If this claim is true – and if we can confirm or substantiate it by objective investigation – then clearly it marks the most important turning point in human history. Bahá'u'lláh says the upheavals and convulsions of today are those foretold in the sacred books of all past religions, that they are preparing the world for the promised era of peace and justice, and that His revelation has set in motion the forces that will gradually bring it about. He has also given to the world approximately one hundred volumes of guidance on how individuals and institutions can best meet the challenges of this time, hastening the Golden Age that must follow.

In deciding whether Bahá'u'lláh's claim merits investigation, we must bear in mind two points.

The first point is that He does not ask anyone to accept a literal interpretation of ancient prophecy. According to Bahá'u'lláh, most prophecies of past religions have important meanings that are to be understood symbolically, not literally. For example, He teaches that the "end of the world" – a recurring theme of scripture – means not the physical destruction of the planet, but rather the end of civilization as we know it through its transformation into a higher, global civilization "with a fullness of life such as the world has never seen nor can as yet conceive." (Shoghi Effendi, PDC 123) This process is viewed not as something magical or instantaneous, but as the result of an unfolding, divinely ordained process of social evolution.

Further examples illustrate this same first point. For instance, Bahá'u'lláh interprets the "return of Christ" (or Buddha, Krishna, or any other Divine Messenger) not as the return of the physical individual but as the mystic return of the Voice of God that spoke through Him. It is, He teaches, the return of the light rather than the lamp, the reappearance in a new human temple of the perfections, power, and authority vested in Christ and the other Divine Educators. Bahá'u'lláh expounds other prophetic themes – resurrection, judgment, and the like – in a similar allegorical manner.

The second, and more important, point is that Bahá'u'lláh does not ask anyone to accept His claim without supporting evidence. Faith is often misunderstood to mean blind acceptance of authority. Bahá'u'lláh denounces this pseudo-faith as "blind imitation" and places the independent investigation of truth in the forefront of His moral principles. Real faith is defined in His teachings to mean conscious knowledge expressed in action. ('Abdu'l-Baha, BWF 383) Although Bahá'u'lláh asks us to take His word for many things, He upholds the right and responsibility of each individual to verify independently His Faith's central premise – namely, that "This thing is not from Me, but from One Who is Almighty and All-Knowing." (PDC 40) He marshals a host of compelling reasons – both logical and intuitive – to support this claim, inviting seekers to "consider His clear evidence" (G 45) and to "gaze, with an open and unbiased mind, on the signs of His Revelation, the proofs of His Mission, and the tokens of His glory." (ibid. 11) ". . . the evidences of His effulgent glory," He writes, "are now actually manifest. It behoveth you to ascertain whether or not such a light hath appeared." (ibid. 103)

My purpose in this book is to "consider His clear evidence" by which we can "ascertain whether or not such a light hath appeared." The details of Bahá'u'lláh's life, the history of His Faith, and the specifics of His teachings will be examined primarily for the light they shed on the central issue: *Who was Bahá'u'lláh?* In other words, was He – as He claimed – the promised World Redeemer foretold in the sacred books of past ages, and is His message a genuine revelation from God?

If the correct answer is "Yes," then clearly it is vital that we know it. Bahá'u'lláh's revelation, if genuine, would enable us to understand the changes shaking the world today, to foresee the results they will produce, and to make the most of the challenges and opportunities they offer.

The second chapter of this book will provide a brief summary of Bahá'í history and of Bahá'u'lláh's major teachings; the third will suggest a few of the many ways an inquirer can test His claim. The remaining chapters will present the actual evidence that supports my own belief as a Bahá'í. Whether my personal reasons seem convincing to others is less important to me than whether they stimulate independent investigation. That, of course, will be for the reader to decide.

Chapter Two
DIVINE SPRINGTIME

We spend our lives trying to unlock the mystery of the universe, but there was a Turkish prisoner, Bahá'u'lláh in 'Akká, Palestine, who had the key.
—Leo Tolstoy

Once to every man and nation
   comes the moment to decide,
      Some great Cause, God's new Messiah . . .
—James Russell Lowell

THIS CHAPTER CONSISTS of three parts: (1) an outline of Bahá'u'lláh's major teachings, (2) a capsule history of His Faith, and (3) further details about the nature of His claim. I will refrain, both in this chapter and the next, from offering any arguments or evidence to support that claim; these will come later. For the moment, my purpose is simply to familiarize the reader with the events and concepts to which any such discussion must refer.

BAHÁ'Í TEACHINGS

Bahá'u'lláh's fundamental teaching is that all human beings are children of one God, who, by successively revealing His will in each of the world's historic faiths, has patiently guided humanity towards spiritual and social maturity. Having passed through infancy and adolescence, humanity is now coming of age. Its collective life is undergoing a profound transformation, akin to that of a caterpillar turning into a butterfly. The product of this metamorphosis must and will be the world's first truly global society.

This pivotal concept – planetary unification as the fruit of humankind's dawning maturity – is the principle Bahá'ís call the "oneness of humanity." As formulated by Bahá'u'lláh in the latter half of the nineteenth century, this principle is much more than a vague platitude. It incorporates a bold and detailed plan for world reconstruction, involving an "organic change" in the very nature of society. When Bahá'u'lláh says "The earth is but one country, and mankind its citizens," (G 250) He means it in every sense of the phrase: political, economic, social, institutional – even military.

All of Bahá'u'lláh's other teachings revolve around the oneness of humanity, as spokes revolve around the hub of a wheel. To support and implement this overriding goal, He calls for widespread application of the following principles:

Independent investigation of truth: Each human being is born with the right and obligation to investigate reality – especially the reality of religion – without undue influence from others. ". . . see with thine own eyes and not through the eyes of others," writes Bahá'u'lláh, "and . . . know of thine own knowledge and not through the knowledge of thy neighbor." (AHW no. 1) "The essence of all that We have revealed for thee is Justice, is for man to free himself from idle fancy and imitation . . . and look into all things with a searching eye." (TB 157)

Acceptance of the divine origin of all world religions: The time has come, Bahá'u'lláh says, for the world's contending faiths to recognize one another as different stages of one ever-evolving religion of God. In every age, God speaks through a chosen mediator, adapting His teaching to the specialized needs of the time and the growing capacity of humanity. Bahá'u'lláh states that despite these outward differences (compounded by many centuries of human misunderstanding and prejudice): "Every true Prophet hath regarded His Message as fundamentally the same as the Revelation of every other Prophet gone before Him." (G 78-9)

Eradication of prejudice in all its forms: Bahá'u'lláh demands vigorous effort, through individual action as well as education and public policy, to abolish the root causes of prejudice. Bahá'ís therefore cherish unity in diversity, cultivating an integrated community life wherein members socialize, work together, and even intermarry across barriers of color, nationality, religion, and social status.

Equal rights and opportunities for men and women: The two sexes are likened in the Bahá'í teachings to two wings that must be balanced before the bird of humanity can soar aloft. In particular, Bahá'u'lláh identifies equal participation by women in government decision-making as a vital key to world peace.

Reconciliation of science and religion: Both disciplines, says Bahá'u'lláh, are different paths to a single truth. Rightly understood, science and religion are therefore in complete harmony, for truth can never contradict itself. 'Abdu'l-Bahá states, "Should a man try to fly with the wing of religion alone he would quickly fall into the quagmire of superstition, whilst on the other hand, with the wing of science alone he would also make no progress, but fall into the despairing slough of materialism." He continues, "When religion, shorn of its superstitions, traditions, and unintelligent dogmas, shows its conformity with science, then will there be a great unifying, cleansing force

22

in the world which will sweep before it all wars, disagreements, discords and struggles. . . ." (PT 143-6)

World peace through collective security: Bahá'u'lláh urges all nations to limit armaments and, by joining in a global federation, unitedly to resist aggression from any member-state. His plan goes far beyond current United Nations activities: He envisages a world constitution, a world parliament, a world court with binding authority to settle disputes among nations, and a world executive to carry out decisions of the parliament and court. While safeguarding the rights and freedoms of all members, such a system – representative self-government on a planetary scale – would empower humanity as a whole to implement its collective will peacefully through international law.

Adoption of a universal auxiliary language: He calls upon the nations to choose, by mutual consent, a single language to be taught in schools throughout the globe in addition to each country's mother tongue. This would provide a powerful tool for international understanding and cooperation while respecting the cultural heritage of all.

Universal compulsory education: This principle is one that Bahá'u'lláh forcefully enunciated long before it became routine policy in most of today's developed nations. Its importance remains tragically underestimated throughout much of the world.

Elimination of extremes of wealth and poverty: Public policy, according to Bahá'u'lláh, must limit dire poverty on the one hand and gross accumulation of excessive wealth on the other. The intent of this principle is to preserve degrees of wealth, which are necessary, while abolishing extremes, which are not. Bahá'u'lláh encourages private initiative while condemning as unjust and unworkable all attempts to impose complete economic equality.

Recognition of love and unity as the central purpose of religion: Bahá'u'lláh categorically forbids not only religious violence but all forms of religious conflict and contention as alien to the true spirit of faith. He states that God's purpose in sending His Messengers has always been to unite human hearts; if religion has the opposite effect, we would be better off without it.

*****

While these themes accurately reflect the spirit of the Bahá'í Faith, they in no way exhaust its teachings. Bahá'u'lláh touches on literally thousands of vital issues, ancient and modern, disclosing in the process a comprehensive blueprint for a unified world society. No summary can capture so vast a

23

panorama of ideas; it can only hint at their scope and direction.

Bahá'u'lláh's teachings emphasize, moreover, that "ideas and principles are helpless without a divine power to put them into effect." (PUP 250) The primary function of divine revelation, He explains, is not to introduce new teachings (important though these are), but to provide such a power. Here is part of what He says about this all-important topic.

The Messengers of God, according to Bahá'u'lláh, are far more than great teachers or reformers. They are Spiritual Suns through Whom God floods the world with divine energy. This intangible yet dynamic influence – traditionally called the Holy Spirit – is the power by which God stirs the Divine Messenger and, through Him, all humanity. The Messenger from God is "luminous in Himself," while all other souls must borrow His light; ('Abdu'l-Bahá, SAQ 154) and His recurring appearance affects human society much as springtime affects the physical world. Whenever a new Messenger "shines upon the worlds of spirits, of thoughts and of hearts, then the spiritual spring and new life appear, the power of the wonderful spring-time becomes visible, and marvelous benefits are apparent." (ibid. 163) New thoughts, new trends, and new movements surface everywhere (even among those unaware of their source in the new revelation), and a universal fermen-tation sweeps away obsolete ideas and institutions. As the mystical impulse generated by the new Messenger gradually penetrates society, it attracts ever-increasing numbers to rally around Him and recognize His divine authority. Sooner or later it culminates in the birth of a new social order based on the newly revealed laws and teachings.

Bahá'ís believe it is this divine impulse that has enabled every past revelation to create a new and higher civilization; it is this, they believe, that ensures the eventual emergence of a world commonwealth based on Bahá'u'-lláh's social principles, and the continued growth and development of that commonwealth under the influence of future Messengers from God. Bahá'u'-lláh indicates, however, that while this divinely ordained process is both irresistible and inevitable, it is not automatic. The social transformation that follows the appearance of a Messenger from God may be relatively quick and benign; it may be exceedingly long and painful; or it may fall somewhere between these extremes. How easily humanity navigates the transition is determined primarily by the readiness of individuals to investigate and accept the new Messenger's divine mandate. Our response also determines the extent to which we as individuals benefit spiritually from the new revelation.

Our expectations concerning the feasibility of Bahá'u'lláh's social reforms will depend greatly on whether we accept the reality of this mystical animating power – the power from which (Bahá'ís believe) the teachings derive their spiritual force. Most of His principles by now command widespread acceptance as desirable goals. Something many people still question, however, is whether such goals can ever be translated into practice. It should be clear that if the Bahá'í program is truly a divine revelation, its aims are attainable because – says 'Abdu'l-Baha – "the power of the Kingdom of God will aid and assist in their realization." (WOB 39)

Another question often raised about the Bahá'í Faith is whether it offers anything really new. The answer is a resounding "Yes." Bahá'u'lláh's broad social principles are, of course, no longer new in the sense of being unfamiliar to the general public (although they were radically new and unfamiliar when He first propounded them in the nineteenth century). They certainly are new, however, in the sense that they are not explicit in the sacred books of any previous religion. When we move beyond broad principles to detailed specifics, we can easily identify many elements of the Faith that are new both in the sense of being still unknown to the public and in that of being unparalleled in previous religions. Bahá'u'lláh set forth detailed new laws and ordinances covering marriage and divorce, burial and inheritance, prayer and fasting, personal conduct and countless other matters; created a revolutionary new type of administrative order designed to implement His laws and principles throughout the world and serve as a pattern for future society; and provided vast amounts of never-before-revealed information concerning God's purpose for humankind, the nature of life after death and how to prepare for it, and many similar topics. His followers believe that this astonishing system of laws, institutions, and doctrines, being of divine rather than human origin, is destined to uplift and regenerate society. Be that as it may, one can hardly deny either the novelty or the originality of the overall structure.

The admitted importance of these two questions – "Is the Bahá'í program really practical?" and "Does it offer anything really new?" – is reflected in the fact that they are frequently asked by persons investigating the religion. For the reasons stated above, I believe the answer, in each case, hinges on a deeper, logically more fundamental issue: *Who was Bahá'u'lláh?* If He was the bearer of a genuine revelation from God, then that revelation must contain much that is both new and practical. To doubt that it does so is to doubt that Bahá'u'lláh Himself is Who He claims to be.

That is why this book will keep the spotlight on the crucial question of Bahá'u'lláh's identity. One must, of course, know something of His teachings in order to gauge the truth or falsity of His claim, and the book will discuss these teachings extensively in connection with that central issue. It also will provide an extensive bibliography for those seeking more information. The point I wish to stress, however, is that one cannot logically investigate the Bahá'í message without reference to the Messenger.

THE HISTORICAL BACKGROUND

Persia (currently called Iran) was in biblical times the heart of a fabulous empire. By the mid-nineteenth century, however, it had entirely lost its ancient glory and was regarded throughout most of the world as backward and insignificant. A reactionary monarchy held absolute sway over a mostly superstitious and apathetic populace; government and people alike were subject, in turn, to the pervasive influence of a fanatical Muslim priesthood. The prevailing religion was the Shí'ih sect of Islam. It was a closed – one might say locked – society, hostile to all progressive ideas and particularly those of the "satanic" West.

It was in this darkened corner of the world that the Bahá'í Faith began in 1844. Its destiny was shaped by the lives of three Central Figures – the Báb, Bahá'u'lláh, and 'Abdu'l-Bahá.

The Báb (1819-50)

On 23 May 1844, Siyyid 'Alí-Muḥammad, a twenty-four-year-old merchant from the Persian city of Shíráz, declared that He was a Messenger from God and the Herald of a still greater Messenger soon to follow. He took the title of the Báb, meaning "Gate," indicating that His mission was to pave the way for the imminent appearance of the Promised One foretold in the holy books of all religions.

The Báb's teaching stirred Persia to its depths, igniting violent opposition from both government and clergy. He was arrested, tortured, imprisoned, and eventually executed by firing squad in Tabríz on 9 July 1850. More than twenty thousand of His followers (known as Bábís) perished in a subsequent bloodbath initiated by authorities in their effort to exterminate His Faith.

The Báb's riddled remains were dumped on the ground outside the city's moat, in the hope they would be eaten by wild animals. His followers, however, risked their lives to rescue His body surreptitiously from careless guards and move it to a safe hiding place. Today it rests in a golden-domed shrine, surrounded by magnificent gardens, on Mount Carmel, at Haifa, Israel.

Bahá'u'lláh (1817-92)

Among the Báb's early followers was Mírzá Ḥusayn-'Alí, later known as Bahá'u'lláh ("the Glory of God"), a title by which the Báb addressed Him. A descendant of Persian royalty and son of a high government official, He inherited great wealth, which He might easily have augmented by taking a position at court. However, He raised many eyebrows by turning away from the halls of power, devoting Himself and His fortune instead to humanitarian service. Upon learning of the Báb's message, Bahá'u'lláh became the movement's most effective and articulate spokesman.

As a highly visible leader of the Bábí community, He was a natural target for the persecution that followed the Báb's martyrdom. In 1852 Bahá'u'lláh was chained, beaten, imprisoned, stripped of His wealth, and marked for death. However, at the last moment, the authorities, fearing awkward repercussions from the slaying of so prominent a figure, decided instead to deport Him and His family to Baghdad, Iraq. (Iraq at that time was part of the Turkish Empire, also known as the Ottoman Empire.)

For a while, the government and clergy felt they had extinguished the Faith of the Báb. Their relief was short-lived, however, as the movement again surged forward under Bahá'u'lláh's now-distant but vigorous leadership. Seeking to remove Him even farther from their borders, Persia prevailed upon the Ottoman government to banish Him again. Bahá'u'lláh and His family were therefore "invited" to Constantinople, capital of the Turkish Empire, where authorities assumed they could watch and control His activities with relative ease.

On the eve of this transfer, in April 1863, Bahá'u'lláh declared to His companions that He was the promised Messenger Whose coming it had been the Báb's mission to announce. Almost all of the Bábís eventually accepted this claim, thereafter becoming known as Bahá'ís.

Bahá'u'lláh's removal to the Ottoman capital, far from silencing Him, had the opposite effect. A cosmopolitan trade-center, Constantinople was a frequent stopover for visiting Persians and other travelers, who carried His teachings far and wide. Moreover, leaders of thought residing in Constantinople itself gravitated increasingly towards Bahá'u'lláh. Though He and His followers shunned political pursuits, Bahá'u'lláh's growing spiritual influence eventually alarmed Turkish officials, already under pressure from the government of Persia to send Him still farther away. Once again He was uprooted and banished, this time to distant Adrianople – the Turkish equivalent of Siberia. This latest countermeasure, however, proved to be simply another exercise in futility; its chief result was to amplify the proclamation of Bahá'u'lláh's message and fan the flames of His Cause. In 1868 His dismayed adversaries responded by locking Him and His retinue in the remote Turkish fortress-prison of 'Akká, now a city in Israel, though at that time within the Ottoman Empire. This punishment was intended as a death sentence, conditions in 'Akká being so foul and inhumane that the hardiest prisoner seldom survived more than a year. Many of Bahá'u'lláh's companions, including His beloved youngest son, Mírzá Mihdí, did perish in the prison; He Himself was strictly confined within the fortress walls for no less than nine years.

Throughout this grim incarceration, Bahá'u'lláh continued guiding His movement to new victories and adding to the already vast collection of His writings. From 'Akká He proclaimed His mission in letters to the kings and rulers of the world, urging them to compose their differences and create a global federation to secure a just and lasting peace. "Had they hearkened unto Me," He later wrote, "they would have beheld the earth another earth." (quoted in PDC 6) Nevertheless, He vowed that God would ensure victory for the Bahá'í Cause, with or without assistance from any king.

The harsh confinement eventually was relaxed as Bahá'u'lláh's character and personality won the friendship of His jailers. Towards the end of His life, though still nominally a prisoner, He was allowed to move about as He pleased, continue His writing, and meet with the many pilgrims and visiting dignitaries who sought His presence.

When He passed away on 29 May 1892, the news reached the Turkish government in a cable opening with the words "the Sun of Bahá has set." (GPB 222) His earthly remains are interred near 'Akká in a shrine at Bahjí (Delight), across the Bay of Haifa from Mount Carmel.

'Abdu'l-Bahá (1844-1921)

Bahá'u'lláh's eldest son, 'Abbás Effendi, was born 23 May 1844 – the night of the Báb's declaration. As He grew to manhood He shared fully in the persecutions that rained upon Bahá'u'lláh, becoming His father's ablest supporter and assistant. Known to Bahá'ís as "the Master," He preferred the title He Himself chose – 'Abdu'l-Bahá, "servant of the Glory." Bahá'u'lláh's last will and testament named 'Abdu'l-Bahá the head and interpreter of the Faith and made His word equal in authority, though not in rank, to Bahá'u'lláh's own.

While still a prisoner in 1898, 'Abdu'l-Bahá greeted the first Western Bahá'í pilgrims to 'Akká. After His release in 1908 He undertook a series of journeys that brought Him in 1911-13 to Europe and America. Here He expounded Bahá'u'lláh's message before large audiences in churches, auditoriums, and private homes; drew extensive press coverage; and met with many leaders of thought.

Returning to Palestine, 'Abdu'l-Bahá received a knighthood from the British Crown for His relief work during World War I, supervised preliminary construction of the Shrine of the Báb, began implementing the Administrative Order envisioned in the writings of Bahá'u'lláh, and designed a long-range teaching plan to carry the Bahá'í Faith throughout the earth.

'Abdu'l-Bahá passed away in 1921 and is interred in a northern room of the Shrine of the Báb in Haifa.

The Bahá'í Administrative Order

Bahá'u'lláh and 'Abdu'l-Bahá provided for continuing leadership of the Faith through two institutions: the Guardianship, a hereditary office holding the exclusive right to interpret authoritatively the Bahá'í teachings; and the Universal House of Justice, a democratically elected body of men empowered to legislate on all questions not covered in the sacred texts.

'Abdu'l-Bahá's will and testament named His grandson Shoghi Effendi the first Guardian of the Cause. Shoghi Effendi worked tirelessly towards the establishment of the Universal House of Justice, which was first elected in 1963. He also produced masterful translations of the Bahá'í sacred writings, wrote extensively on the administration, history, and goals of the Faith, completed the Shrine of the Báb, shepherded the construction of America's first Bahá'í House of Worship, and launched the successive teaching campaigns planned by 'Abdu'l-Bahá. When he died in 1957 at the age of sixty-one, he had no children and was unable to appoint a successor under the terms of 'Abdu'l-Bahá's will; there is thus no incumbent to the Guardianship. Although this development came as a shock to the Bahá'ís, it had been envisioned and provided for in Bahá'u'lláh's book of laws, the Kitáb-i-Aqdas (Most Holy Book). (See Bahá'u'lláh's statement from the Kitáb-i-Aqdas, quoted in *Messages From the Universal House of Justice* ¶75.13, p. 159.) The Universal House of Justice, in keeping with those provisions, today directs the Faith from the Bahá'í World Center in Haifa.

Local and national Bahá'í affairs are administered by a network of Spiritual Assemblies, each consisting of nine believers elected without regard to gender, race, class, or other social or economic distinction. Elections are by secret ballot, with no campaigns or nominations; and the religion has no clergy, paid or otherwise. Financial support is accepted only from declared believers, all contributions being both voluntary and confidential.

As part of their global teaching effort, Bahá'ís have sought consistently to disperse throughout the world. As a result, though there are relatively few large concentrations of Bahá'ís, the Faith has become the second most widely spread religion on earth, with a significant following in more countries than any other except Christianity. (The *Encyclopaedia Britannica* yearbook, in successive editions beginning with 1988, lists Christianity as first with 254 countries, the Bahá'í Faith as second with 205, and Islam as third with 172.) Moreover, the Faith exhibits extraordinary cultural and ethnic diversity and rapidly accelerating growth. Its broadly based unity has made it an effective champion of such causes as international peace, women's rights, social and economic development, environmental conservation, and literacy training.

THE MANIFESTATION OF GOD

Only by clearly understanding Bahá'u'lláh's claim can we decide how best to evaluate it. To better grasp the specifics of that claim, let us now consider what Bahá'u'lláh says about the nature of God and His Messengers.

Bahá'u'lláh teaches that there are three distinct planes of existence or levels of reality: the world of God, the world of humanity, and the world of the Messengers (or "Manifestations") Who mediate between God and humanity. A few comments are in order about each of these worlds.

Regarding the highest plane of existence, Bahá'u'lláh "proclaims unequivocally the existence and oneness of a personal God, unknowable, inaccessible, the source of all Revelation, eternal, omniscient, omnipresent and almighty." (Shoghi Effendi GPB 139) The God thus described "is a God Who is conscious of His creation, Who has a Mind, a Will, a Purpose, and not, as many scientists and materialists believe, an unconscious and deter-mined force operating in the universe. . . . To say that God is a personal Reality does not mean that He has a physical form, or does in any way resemble a human being. To entertain such belief would be sheer blas-phemy." (on behalf of Shoghi Effendi 29 April 1939; quoted in LG 478) Bahá'u'lláh writes that God is "immeasurably exalted beyond every human attribute such as corporeal existence, ascent and descent, egress and regress. . . . He is, and hath ever been, veiled in the ancient eternity of His Essence, and will remain in His Reality everlastingly hidden from the sight of men." (WOB 113)

At the other end of the spectrum is the human world. Bahá'u'lláh states that God created all humanity "to know Him and to love Him" (G 65) and "to carry forward an ever-advancing civilization." (ibid. 215) Moreover, every human being is created in "the image and likeness of God" (cf. Genesis 1:25-6) – not in any physical sense (for God has no physical form), but in the sense of being able to express God's attributes such as knowledge, love, mercy, justice, kindness, will, loftiness, and countless others.

However, finite man cannot conceive or comprehend the Infinite Creator, nor can he reflect God's attributes except within the limits of his own capacity. He is able, at best, to make continual progress towards perfection without ever actually achieving it. Moreover, he cannot do even this much by his own unaided effort, since he has no direct access to the knowledge of God or His will. God therefore intervenes periodically in history, at intervals typically varying from five hundred to one thousand years, provid-ing humankind with guidance through a chosen Christ-figure or Manifes-tation.

Bahá'u'lláh teaches that "this subtle, this mysterious and ethereal Being" (G 66), the Manifestation of God, has two aspects – one human, the other divine. His human personality is "in the uttermost state of servitude, a servitude the like of which no man can possibly attain." (KI 179) His inner reality, however, manifests the infinite perfections of God as a polished mirror reflects the image of the sun. He is a relay station linking the world of God with that of man. This unique capacity is a divine gift that cannot be acquired by study or effort: "However far the disciples might progress, they could never become Christ." ('Abdu'l-Baha, SAQ 233-4)The Divine Manifestation belongs to a different sphere altogether.

Elaborating this theme, Bahá'u'lláh writes that God

"hath manifested unto men the Day Stars of His divine guidance . . . and hath ordained the knowledge of these sanctified Beings to be identical with the knowledge of His own Self. . . . Every one of them is the Way of God that connecteth this world with the realms above, and the Standard of His Truth unto every one in the kingdoms of earth and heaven." (G 50)

"These sanctified Mirrors, these Day Springs of ancient glory are, one and all, the Exponents on earth of Him Who is the central Orb of the universe, its Essence and ultimate Purpose. From Him proceed their knowledge and power; from Him is derived their sovereignty. . . . These Tabernacles of Holiness, these Primal Mirrors which reflect the light of unfading glory, are but expressions of Him Who is the Invisible of the Invisibles. . . . these illuminated Souls . . . have, each and every one of them, been endowed with all the attributes of God, such as sovereignty, dominion, and the like, even though to outward seeming they be shorn of all earthly majesty." (ibid. 47-9)

In saying the Manifestations are "endowed with all the attributes of God," Bahá'u'lláh means just that. God is the All-Knowing; the Manifestations are therefore "omniscient at will." (Shoghi Effendi, UD 449) God is the All-Powerful; for the Manifestations, therefore, "any difficult or impracticable thing is possible and easy . . . for They have all power." ('Abdu'l-Baha, SAQ 100-2) God is infallible; consequently, "whatever proceeds from them is identical with the truth, and conformable to reality." (ibid. 173) God is love; He is the source of all goodness and perfection; the Manifestations are therefore "the supreme embodiment of all that is lovable." (Bahá'u'lláh, GPB 119)These divine qualities notwithstanding, the Messengers of God also are fully human – a duality often reflected in Their utterances. Sometimes the Manifestation speaks from His human position, evincing complete humility and self-effacement. At other times, His human personality fades into the background, leaving only "the Voice of Divinity, the Call of God Himself." (G 55) These two modes of speech may alternate within a single discourse, or even engage in dialogue with each other. In one of His prayers Bahá'u'lláh expresses this delightful paradox:

> *"When I contemplate, O my God, the relationship that bindeth me to Thee, I am moved to proclaim to all created things 'verily I am God!'; and when I consider my own self, lo, I find it coarser than clay!"* (WOB 113)

Bahá'u'lláh's claim to fulfill prophecies of Christ, Buddha, and other Divine Messengers in no way exalts Him above His predecessors. Though Their revelations vary according to the receptivity of the age, no Manifestation is intrinsically superior to another. So perfect is their inward spiritual unity that they may – He writes – be "regarded as one soul and the same person. . . . They all abide in the same tabernacle, soar in the same heaven, are seated upon the same throne, utter the same speech, and proclaim the same Faith." (ibid. 115)

Moreover, the Bahá'í Faith "emphatically repudiates the claim to be regarded as the final revelation of God's will and purpose for mankind." (Shoghi Effendi, ibid.) Bahá'u'lláh specifically affirms:

> *"God hath sent down His Messengers to succeed to Moses and Jesus, and He will continue to do so till 'the end that hath no end'; so that His grace may, from the heaven of Divine bounty, be continually vouchsafed to mankind."* (ibid. 116)

He does state, however, that a period of at least one thousand years must separate His revelation from the one to follow. (*Synopsis* 14)

From these and many similar statements, we can see that there is nothing vague or ambiguous about the claim of Bahá'u'lláh. It is simple in concept, detailed and specific in its implications, and awesome in its magnitude.

We turn now to the problem of evaluating that claim. What kind of evidence might have a bearing on its truth? What credentials could a Manifestation offer that would vindicate His mission, and how might we verify them? These are, of course, subtle and intricate questions – yet they lie directly in our path. Before discussing any specific evidence in connection with Bahá'u'lláh's claim, let us try in the next chapter to map out a strategy for collecting such evidence and testing its validity.

Chapter Three
LIFE'S LABORATORY

... the years of searching in the dark for a truth that one feels, but cannot express; the intense desire and the alternations of confidence and misgiving, until one breaks through to clarity and understanding, are only known to him who has himself experienced them.

—*Albert Einstein*

Faith . . . plucks at a twig of evidence.

—*Emily Dickinson*

WE CANNOT LOGICALLY JUSTIFY a claim of authority by invoking the very authority in question. Such an approach would commit the fallacy of circular reasoning. However, it would be pointless for an invisible Deity to reveal His will through a human envoy unless He also furnished clues or indications enabling us to recognize that envoy.

Bahá'u'lláh assures us that God can and does provide such signs. He states that it would be "far from the grace of the All-Bountiful and from His loving providence and tender mercies" to send His Messenger with incomplete identification, while holding humanity accountable for failure to accept Him (KI 14). 'Abdu'l-Bahá, who defines faith as conscious knowledge expressed through good deeds (BWF 383), rejects "blind imitation" as a basis for such acceptance. "You must come into the knowledge of the divine Manifestations and Their teachings through proofs and evidences" (PUP 227), He says, indicating that those who seek such knowledge have at their disposal "every manner of evidence, whether based on reason or on the text of the scriptures and traditions" (WOB 127-8).

But what constitutes evidence? How do we know that any particular statement is true? For simple questions, such as whether it is raining outside, there is no problem: We simply look and see for ourselves. If we are not in a position to look, we ask someone else. Sometimes we can look up answers in a book; this works well for things such as telephone numbers or the height of Mount Everest.

When we confront the truly pivotal questions of life, however, we must work out the answers for ourselves. If there is such a thing as divine revelation, then the soul's response to that revelation is easily the most vital issue anyone will ever confront. Certainly we should benefit from the insights and experiences of others in this connection – but it is our destiny, not theirs, that is affected; and it is we, not they, who will bear ultimate responsibility for our own actions. For all the really important questions – questions such as "Who was Bahá'u'lláh?" – we are on our own. There is too much at stake to gamble on someone else's judgment.

Nor can there be any rigid formula for assessing Bahá'u'lláh's authenticity. There are as many ways as there are individuals, and the way that works for one will not necessarily work for another. Also, we should stipulate at the outset that there is no way to "prove" the claim of Bahá'u'lláh in the sense of providing an ironclad, unchallengeable guarantee: One cannot force a skeptic to accept it; the evidence will not demonstrate it with mathematical certainty, nor is there any way to rule out every conceivable alternative. Proof in this absolute sense does not exist even in the physical sciences, much less in so sensitive and personal an area as religion.

These reservations notwithstanding, there is every reason to press on with our investigation. If absolute certainty is beyond our reach, perhaps a high degree of relative certainty is not. It is instructive to consider, by way of comparison, how conviction is obtained in science.

The Scientific Method

Science insists that since we have no absolute guarantee of truth, it is essential that we test every important proposition in as many ways as possible. There are, as 'Abdu'l-Bahá points out, four ways of testing or judging any conclusion: sense perception, reason, intuition, and authority. Scientists freely use all four. They use their senses (perhaps extended by instruments such as microscopes and telescopes) to gather and verify raw data. They use reason to formulate explanatory ideas and ferret out implications for further testing. Contrary to the stereotype of the cold-blooded technician, scientists rely heavily on intuition (insight, inspiration, gut feeling, the "still small voice" – call it what you will): Every great scientist has a highly developed sixth sense, which may manifest itself in flashes of insight while meditating on a knotty problem or in hunches as to which lines of research are most likely to bear fruit. As to authority, a scientist will be as quick as anyone else to look up needed facts in a reference book and – all other things being equal – will prefer conclusions that fit smoothly into the framework of knowledge already generally accepted as verified.

Scientists realize that each of these four criteria, used by itself, is flawed. The human senses are notoriously prone to error. Reason, unguided by intuition and unchecked by observation, is sterile and frequently misleading.

Valid intuition can be hard to distinguish from mere prejudice or wishful thinking. The voice of authority is suspect until we have verified its credentials and understood its pronouncements; to do either, we must rely on our own fallible minds and hearts. Nevertheless, by applying in concert all the criteria at our disposal, we can obtain conclusions that, while not absolute, are highly reliable. Once we reduce uncertainty to a practical minimum, it even serves a useful purpose: Our awareness of it creates an exhilarating incentive to keep our minds and hearts open and thus to grow continually in knowledge.

The goal of science is to explain reality as we encounter it. This being so, scientific method may be defined as the systematic *testing* of proposed *explanations* (hypotheses) using *data* derived from *experience*. Nothing in the nature of science compels us to define experience in narrow physical terms: It includes whatever is knowable through any legitimate human faculty (these being, as stated, sense perception, reason, intuition, and validated authority). As a practical matter, however, the experience must be potentially *public* – that is, open to repetition by peers. Simply stated, a scientific explanation in any field is one that can be validated by means of open experience.

Now validity, like certainty, is a somewhat subjective and relative concept – a matter of degree. The explanation preferred by scientists as most valid will generally be that which best satisfies two criteria: (1) it must account for the widest range of phenomena using the simplest model and (2) it must correctly predict specific, testable results for our observations of those phenomena.

Long before astronauts could view the earth from space, human beings knew beyond any reasonable doubt that the planet's approximate shape was that of a globe or sphere. Why? Because the spherical-earth theory is the simplest model that predicts all the relevant facts we observe and experience. The theory implies, for instance, that a departing ship should disappear by sinking slowly below the horizon and that the North Star should appear higher in northern countries than in southern ones. These predictions match what we see – a fact well known to the ancient Greeks, among others. Some predictions of the theory could not be tested at once; for example, it implies that a traveler who continues far enough in any direction should return eventually to his starting point. When Magellan circumnavigated the globe, he provided an important confirmation of the spherical-earth theory.

Many predictions of a new idea are not necessarily obvious at first sight. Aristotle cleverly worked out a hidden implication of the spherical-earth theory. Knowing already that a lunar eclipse is the earth's shadow against the moon, cast by the sun from below the earth, he realized that a flat, coin-shaped body must at times cast an oval shadow. On the other hand, he reasoned, a sphere must always cast a circular shadow. By watching eclipses and checking ancient records, Aristotle verified that the earth's shadow is the ever-circular type cast only by a globe. On this basis, plus observations of the North Star and vanishing ships, Aristotle and other Greek philosophers concluded correctly that the earth is spherical.

A critically important step, then, in assessing a scientific proposition is uncovering its predictions: What does it imply that we can test using sense perception, reason, intuition, and authority? Once we answer this question, we know what to look for. In most cases, the easiest way to validate a correct explanation is by striving, with an open mind, to disprove its predictions. If it stands up under fire, we learn to trust it. Astrophysicist Stephen Hawking explains that any theory of physics

". . . is always provisional, in the sense that it is only a hypothesis: You can never prove it. No matter how many times the results of experiments agree with some theory, you can never be sure that the next time the result will not contradict the theory. On the other hand, you can disprove a theory by finding even a single observation that disagrees with the predictions of the theory. As philosopher of science Karl Popper has emphasized, a good theory is characterized by the fact that it makes a number of predictions that could in principle be disproved or falsified by observation. Each time new experiments are observed to agree with the predictions the theory survives, and our confidence in it is increased; but if ever a new observation is found to disagree, we have to abandon or modify the theory. At least that is what is supposed to happen, but you can always question the competence of the person who carried out the observation." (*Brief History of Time* 10)

As Hawking's last comment shows, scientific method is simpler in principle than in practice. A scientist may succeed (if at all) only after a period of deep perplexity, not unlike the "dark night of the soul" that saints and mystics describe as a normal stage of spiritual growth. While scientific method will not relieve us of this struggle, it will help us approach the struggle in a disciplined manner: It may suggest fresh and creative ways to proceed when our quest falters, and it provides a way to judge whether we have reached our goal. If a simple, elegant explanatory model accounts for a large number of facts that previously seemed unrelated, correctly predicts a variety of surprising and unexpected new findings, and survives our systematic attempts to disprove it, then we have every right to place our confidence in it. This is the meaning of "scientific proof," insofar as the term has any meaning at all. The confidence one attains by this method corresponds closely to that sense of certitude known in religion as "faith."

This method is available to all of us, not only to scientists. It is useful in evaluating any proposition, not only those describing physical reality. It calls forth our full range of problem-solving resources – spiritual and emotional as well as material. Scientific method, in its broadest sense, is not a technical procedure; it is a coherent way of thinking and feeling about life itself.

Revelation as a Testable Hypothesis

Now suppose we wish to test – as a scientific hypothesis – Bahá'u'lláh's claim that He is a direct channel of communication from an all-knowing, infallible Supreme Being. It is admittedly hard to imagine any single all-purpose test that could establish such a hypothesis to everyone's satisfaction.

On the other hand, the hypothesis, if untrue, should be fairly easy to discredit. Bahá'u'lláh's recorded utterances fill at least one hundred volumes, of which He states: ". . . out of My mouth proceedeth naught but the essence of truth, which the Lord your God hath revealed." (G 328) Such a claim surely entails consequences that anyone can test using observation and reason.

Here are a few indications one might consider: Bahá'u'lláh made many detailed prophecies. Have these been fulfilled, or have any been contradicted by subsequent events? He described scientific facts that were unknown in His lifetime. Have these been verified, or have any been decisively refuted? He says His words have a unique creative power to facilitate spiritual growth. Can we, by reading and reflecting on those words, experience such a power? We would expect a divinely perfect Being to make an extraordinary impression on those with whom He came into contact. What effect did Bahá'u'lláh have on those around Him? He dictated His books and letters at high speed, never pausing to revise or think, and often with no opportunity for premeditation. Was He able spontaneously to create finished works of consistent excellence, as revelation logically should be? Or do these writings (however brilliant they may be overall) show the wide variations in quality one would expect of a human author composing extemporaneously? He claimed to possess innate, inspired knowledge. Did He have any opportunity, through schooling or self-study, to acquire the skills and knowledge He displayed? These are a few of the ways we can test Bahá'u'lláh's claim. With a little imagination, we can find many others.

We cannot necessarily validate so challenging a claim on the basis of any single test. Suppose, however, we find that the more tests we devise, and the more we widen our investigation, and the more deeply we probe, the more consistent all our findings prove to be with the hypothesis of Bahá'u'-lláh's authenticity? At some point, might not our experiences and observations justify interpreting His claim as "true beyond a reasonable doubt"? Any individual can make such an investigation; and no one, without having done so, can fairly prejudge its outcome. This book is the record of one such investigation. It systematically explores every avenue of inquiry I can think of by which we might test Bahá'u'lláh's claim. It argues that the resulting evidence – which might easily have contradicted that claim – instead supports it in every instance. None of this evidence will constitute "absolute proof": To repeat, it will not necessarily convince a determined skeptic, demonstrate Bahá'u'lláh's authenticity in the manner of a mathematical theorem, or exclude all conceivable alternative hypotheses. What it does mean is that the model which most simply explains and most completely predicts everything we can discover about Bahá'u'lláh is that which accepts His claim as true. If this is correct, then we have as sound a basis for faith in Bahá'u'lláh as we have for faith in any well-established scientific theory.

Chapter Four
BAHÁ'U'LLÁH'S PROPHECIES

A tempest, unprecedented in its violence, unpredictable in its course, catastrophic in its immediate effects, unimaginably glorious in its ultimate consequences, is at present sweeping the face of the earth. . . . The powerful operations of this titanic upheaval are comprehensible to none except such as have recognized the claims of both Bahá'u'lláh and the Báb.

—Shoghi Effendi

Most of the things that have happened in the last fifty years have been fantastic, and it is only by assuming that they will continue to be so that we have any hope of anticipating the future.

—Arthur C. Clarke

THE WORD "PREDICTION" means one thing in science, another in religion. When we study religion scientifically, it is important to distinguish between these meanings. In science, a prediction is any testable inference we draw from a hypothesis or theory. It may equally well describe a future event, a past observation, or an ongoing process. In religion, a prediction generally is a prophecy – a glimpse of the future disclosed through the words of a prophet. Although the scientific and religious meanings may sometimes overlap, they are not identical.

Bearing this distinction in mind, let us consider a scientific prediction (testable inference from a hypothesis) involving religious predictions (prophecies): If Bahá'u'lláh truly was a Manifestation of God, then He should have been able to foretell coming events. To someone who is omniscient at will and free from all error, the future must be an open book.

This practical consequence of Bahá'u'lláh's revelation-claim is something we can test on the basis of observation, reason, intuition, and credible authority. As with any good scientific deduction, we can search for evidence to disprove it. "When a prophet speaketh in the name of the Lord," says the Old Testament, "if the thing follow not, nor come to pass, that is the thing which the Lord hath not spoken. . . ." (Deut. 18:21-2) Note how completely this approach agrees with modern scientific method: The Bible does not suggest that a single correct prophecy (or even several such) would constitute "proof" of a Manifestation's claim. All it says is that a demonstrable *in*ability

39

to make such prophecies would *discredit* that claim. The obvious corollary, however, is that if someone claiming divine inspiration makes a great many specific, seemingly improbable, testable prophecies – prophecies whose non-fulfillment would undermine our confidence – and they invariably come true, then we can hardly fail to be impressed. Two equally reasonable people may differ as to how much any given prophecy bolsters such a claim or how many "hits" should be required to sustain a positive verdict. At some point, however, we might well find it more reasonable to accept that claim than to go on reserving judgment.

Foremost among the "clearest proofs" which Bahá'u'lláh says "attest the truth of His Cause" is the fact that "the prophecies He, in an unmistakable language, hath made have been fulfilled." (G 58) Elsewhere He writes:

"We have laid bare the divine mysteries and in most explicit language foretold future events, that neither the doubts of the faithless, nor the denials of the froward, nor the whisperings of the heedless may keep back the seekers after truth from the Source of the light of the One true God." (TB 241)

"... most of the things which have come to pass on this earth have been announced and prophesied by the Most Sublime Pen ... All that hath been sent down hath and will come to pass, word for word, upon earth. No possibility is left for anyone either to turn aside or protest." (ESW 148-150)

An impartial examination of such prophecies in light of subsequent events will either confirm or falsify these assertions.

In this inquiry we must consider not only the prophecies written or spoken by Bahá'u'lláh Himself, but those of His Forerunner, the Báb, and His Successor, 'Abdu'l-Bahá. The Báb was more than simply a Herald of Bahá'u'lláh. He claimed to be – and was recognized by Bahá'u'lláh as – the bearer in His own right of independent divine revelation. 'Abdu'l-Bahá was not a direct revealer of God's words in the same sense. He was, however, appointed by Bahá'u'lláh as the authorized Interpreter of Bahá'í teachings, which He was empowered to elaborate at will with unerring divine protection. By investing the Báb and 'Abdu'l-Bahá with such authority, Bahá'u'lláh implicitly embraced their teachings and prophecies as His own – increasing both His own burden and our opportunity to test His validity. Most of the predictions cited below are from Bahá'u'lláh's own words, while a few are from the Báb or 'Abdu'l-Bahá. All, however, are Bahá'u'lláh's either directly or indirectly, since all bear His endorsement.

What are the events that have, in Bahá'u'lláh's words, "come to pass on this earth" after being "announced and prophesied by the Most Sublime Pen" in "an unmistakable language"? Consider the following list, compiled from the writings of Bahá'u'lláh and the commentaries of 'Abdu'l-Bahá:

1) The fall from power of the French Emperor Napoleon III and the consequent loss of his empire.
2) The defeat of Germany in two bloody wars, resulting in the "lamentations of Berlin".
3) The success and stability of Queen Victoria's reign.
4) The dismissal of 'Álí Páshá, prime minister of Turkey.
5) The overthrow and murder of Sultan 'Abdu'l-'Azíz of Turkey.
6) The breakup of the Ottoman Empire, leading to the extinction of the "outward splendor" of its capital, Constantinople.
7) The downfall of Násiri'd-Dín Sháh, the Persian monarch.
8) The advent of constitutional government in Persia.
9) A massive (albeit temporary) decline in the fortunes of monarchy throughout the world.
10) A worldwide erosion of ecclesiastical authority.
11) The collapse of the Muslim Caliphate.
12) The spread of communism, the "Movement of the Left", and its rise to world power.
13) The catastrophic decline of that same movement, triggered by the collapse of its egalitarian economy.
14) The rise of Israel as a Jewish homeland.
15) The persecution of Jews on the European continent (the Nazi holocaust).
16) America's violent racial struggles.
17) Bahá'u'lláh's release from the prison of 'Akká and the pitching of His tent on Mount Carmel.
18) The seizure and desecration of Bahá'u'lláh's House in Baghdad.
19) The failure of all attempts to create schism within the Bahá'í Faith.
20) The explosive acceleration of scientific and technological progress.
21) The development of nuclear weapons.
22) The achievement of transmutation of elements, the age-old alchemist's dream.
23) Dire peril for all humanity as a result of that achievement.
24) The discovery that complex elements evolve in nature from simpler ones.
25) The recognition of planets as a necessary by-product of star formation.
26) Space travel.
27) The realization that some forms of cancer are communicable.
28) Failure to find evidence for a "missing link" between man and ape.

29) The non-existence of a mechanical ether (the supposed light-carrying substance posited by classical physics), and its redefinition as an abstract reality.
30) The breakdown of mechanical models (literal images) as a basis for understanding the physical world.

We will now discuss these predictions, showing when and how each one was made and the circumstances by which each was fulfilled. First, however, let us consider their common historical setting.

TABLETS TO THE KINGS

Shortly before reaching the prison-city of 'Akká in 1868, and continuing for several years thereafter, Bahá'u'lláh, in words of supreme majesty, announced the inception of the long-awaited "Kingdom of God on Earth". To the world's reigning monarchs He addressed a series of letters (also known as "Tablets"), setting forth His claims and the highlights of God's plan whereby the nations could fulfil the vision of Isaiah: "They shall beat their swords into plowshares, and their spears into pruninghooks . . . neither shall they learn war any more." (Isa. 2:4) Bahá'u'lláh addressed similar letters collectively to these same rulers and heads of state, as well as to leaders of religion, various segments of society, and humanity in general.

In these Tablets Bahá'u'lláh declared that human society was about to be revolutionized by the birth of a divine and world-embracing civilization. "The whole earth", He exclaimed, "is now in a state of pregnancy. The day is approaching when it will have yielded its noblest fruits, when from it will have sprung forth the loftiest trees, the most enchanting blossoms, the most heavenly blessings." (PDC 5) This mighty transformation, He said, would come about through historical forces which God had irreversibly set in motion and which the kings could resist or ignore only at their own peril. He advised them to "have mercy on yourselves and on those beneath you" (ibid. 23) by joining forces to bring about the unity of humankind.

Every birth, however glorious its outcome, is a potentially grueling ordeal preceded by sharp labor pains. The birth of a new civilization is no exception. Bahá'u'lláh indicated to the kings that their response would largely determine the difficulty of the coming transition. He outlined three possible choices: (1) They could investigate His claim, acknowledge Him as the promised Inaugurator of God's kingdom, and establish in His lifetime what He called the "Most Great Peace" – that earthly paradise in which "the earth shall be filled with the knowledge of the Lord, as the waters cover the sea" (Isa. 11:9). (2) Rejecting His claim, the kings might still establish at once the "Lesser Peace", a strictly political plan to abolish war through a worldwide system of representative self-government. Although this stopgap measure would not in itself heal the deeper spiritual maladies afflicting humanity, it would make such healing possible by paving the way for the long-range establishment of the Most Great Peace. (3) They could reject both the proposals outlined above. In that case God, working through the ordinary masses, would in His own time still bring about both the Lesser and the Most Great Peace. The immediate result, however, would be "convulsions and chaos" (PDC 116) on a scale hitherto unimaginable.

Within this broad context, Bahá'u'lláh offered specific advice to individual rulers and, in so doing, made a number of detailed prophecies. The most important of these letters were compiled in a book entitled *Súriy-i-Haykal* (Discourse of the Temple), published in 1869 in Bombay and later reprinted several times. Many of the prophecies I will cite appeared in that book; all were published and widely circulated in advance of the events to which they refer.

Napoleon III

PROPHECY 1: *The fall from power of the French Emperor Napoleon III and the consequent loss of his empire.*

Bahá'u'lláh warned Napoleon III, emperor of France, that "thy kingdom shall be thrown into confusion, and thine empire shall pass from thine hands . . . Commotions shall seize all the people in that land . . . We see abasement hastening after thee . . ." (PDC 30) This dire prediction, defying conventional wisdom, came true within a year of its publication, as a result of the Franco-Prussian War of 1870. Napoleon's empire did indeed "pass from" his hands; he himself was taken prisoner and exiled to England, where he died in "abasement" two years later.

Germany

PROPHECY 2: *The defeat of Germany in two bloody wars, resulting in the "lamentations of Berlin".*

To Napoleon's jubilant conqueror, Kaiser William I of Germany, Bahá'u'lláh then disclosed that country's grim future. He foresaw the "banks of the Rhine . . . covered with gore, inasmuch as the swords of retribution were drawn against you . . . And we hear the lamentations of Berlin, though she be today in conspicuous glory". He added ominously that Germany would have "another turn" at bloody defeat (PDC 37). Interpreting this and other prophecies of His father, 'Abdu'l-Bahá stated in 1912 that the imminent struggle would "set aflame the whole of Europe" and that "By 1917 kingdoms will fall and cataclysms will rock the earth." (BNE 65) After this part of the prediction materialized in World War I (1914-18), He wrote that the "vanquished Powers" would "rekindle the flame of war" (WOB 30) and that the inevitable next conflict would be "fiercer than the last" (WOB 46). World War II handed Germany its second and still greater loss, while both defeats brought retributive sanctions resulting in decades of agonizing "lamentations" for Berlin.

Queen Victoria

PROPHECY 3: *The success and stability of Queen Victoria's reign.*
    Whereas the French and German rulers had been widely perceived as unstoppable, the reign of England's Queen Victoria was generally viewed as precarious and uncertain. Bahá'u'lláh again challenged the pundits: He informed the Queen that God had smiled upon her just and humanitarian policies and that, as a result, "the foundations of the edifice of thine affairs will be strengthened, and the hearts of all that are beneath thy shadow, whether high or low, will be tranquillized." (PDC 36) Britain did indeed prosper under her administration, which lasted until 1901, fully justifying Bahá'u'lláh's bright forecast.

The Crown of Turkey

PROPHECY 4: *The dismissal of 'Álí Páshá as prime minister of Turkey.*
PROPHECY 5: *The overthrow and murder of Sultan 'Abdu'l-'Azíz of Turkey.*
    In a Tablet revealed and circulated around 1870 Bahá'u'lláh foretold that God would soon "dismiss" 'Álí Páshá, the entrenched and vastly powerful prime minister of Ottoman Turkey, then "lay hold on" Sultan 'Abdu'l-'Azíz, the tyrannical "Chief who ruleth the land" (PDC 62). The Arabic expression "lay hold on" is a figure of speech implying violent and untimely death – a meaning rendered especially portentous by Bahá'u'lláh's added warning to the sultan himself that he stood in grave danger of betrayal by faithless subordinates (G 232-3). So impossible did these prophecies sound at the time that they were publicized by Bahá'u'lláh's adversaries in an attempt to discredit Him. A few years later, however, the abrupt dismissal of 'Álí Páshá, followed by an 1876 palace coup resulting in the overthrow and subsequent assassination of 'Abdu'l-'Azíz, fulfilled the prophecies to the last word.

The Ottoman Empire

PROPHECY 6: *The breakup of the Ottoman Empire, leading to the extinction of the "outward splendor" of its capital, Constantinople.*

Bahá'u'lláh also turned His prophetic spotlight from the Ottoman rulers to the Turkish Empire itself: "Soon", He told them, ". . . sedition will be stirred up in your midst, and your dominions will be disrupted . . . Be expectant . . . Erelong will ye behold that which hath been sent down from the Pen of My command." (PDC 61) He described a series of nightmarish disasters "ready to overtake" the empire and drive it to its knees. During the course of these catastrophes, He wrote, Adrianople would "pass out of the hands of the king"; the "outward splendor" of the imperial capital, Constantinople, would "perish" (PDC 61-2); and conditions would "wax so grievous, that the very sands on the desolate hills will moan, and the trees on the mountain will weep, and blood will flow out of all things." (PDC 61) These dire predictions were more than justified by a seemingly endless succession of invasions, wars, epidemics, famines, massacres and revolutions in which nine-tenths of the Turkish army died or deserted and a quarter of the populace perished. Adrianople was occupied by Russian troops. The once-vast Turkish empire was shriveled into a tiny Asiatic republic, while its capital, Constantinople, was abandoned by its conquerors and indeed stripped of its "outward splendor".

Náṣiri'd-Dín Sháh

PROPHECY 7: *The downfall of Náṣiri'd-Dín Sháh, the Persian monarch.*

Náṣiri'd-Dín Sháh, ruler of Bahá'u'lláh's native Persia, was a callous dictator to whom policies of genocide and blood-curdling torture seemed second nature. Bahá'u'lláh wrote of him and others like him: "God hath not blinked . . . at the tyranny of the oppressor. More particularly in this Revelation He hath visited each and every tyrant with His vengeance." (GPB 224) He added that Náṣiri'd-Dín, being the "Prince of Oppressors", was therefore destined to become an "object-lesson for the world" (GPB 225). This stroke fell on 1 May 1896, the eve of his fiftieth anniversary Jubilee, when Náṣiri'd-Dín died at the hand of a terrorist hired by a political adversary (who also was, incidentally, a prominent persecutor of the Bahá'í Faith). Since the shooting occurred while the sháh was away from the capital, his ministers – desperate to suppress the news – propped up his corpse in the royal carriage during the return trip, hoping that the watching public would assume all was well.

45

The Persian Constitution

PROPHECY 8: *The advent of constitutional government in Persia.*

Bahá'u'lláh had also predicted, in the early 1870s, that the "reins of power" in Persia would soon "fall into the hands of the people" (G 111). No political analyst of His time could have taken such a prophecy seriously, since age-old Persian culture and tradition required that its sovereign wield godlike power, unhampered by constitutional constraints or public participation. However, the murder of Náṣiri'd-Dín Sháh signaled the start of a movement to curb the powers of the monarchy. This movement, slowly gathering steam, plunged the country into a Constitutional Revolution spanning 1906 to 1911. After a bitter and at times violent struggle, the monarchy was forced to concede much of its authority to the new parliament. Although the Peacock Throne remained in place until Persia's Islamic Revolution of 1979, its occupants never again enjoyed the unfettered prerogatives of Náṣiri'd-Dín and his predecessors.

OTHER PROPHECIES

When His claims and His peace proposals both went unheeded, Bahá'u'lláh reiterated His warning of dire consequences. "The winds of despair are, alas, blowing from every direction," He wrote, "and the strife that divides and afflicts the human race is daily increasing. The signs of impending convulsions and chaos can now be discerned, inasmuch as the prevailing order appears to be lamentably defective." (PDC 116) Many of His further prophecies elaborated this insight.

Bahá'u'lláh noted that those with the most to lose from the coming upheaval were the ones whose negligence had brought it about: namely, the world's secular and religious leaders. He stated that God, holding them accountable for their conduct, would therefore strip them of influence: "From two ranks amongst men power hath been seized: kings and ecclesiastics." (PDC 71)

Monarchy

PROPHECY 9: *A massive (albeit temporary) decline in the fortunes of monarchy throughout the world.*

In His general letters to the kings of East and West, Bahá'u'lláh warned that if they ignored His advice, a resistless "Divine chastisement" would overwhelm them (PDC 23). Absolute monarchy – the standard and time-honored mode of government during Bahá'u'lláh's lifetime – has since been transformed by a rising tide of calamities into the quaint relic of a bygone age.

Ecclesiasticism

PROPHECY 10: *A worldwide erosion of ecclesiastical authority.*
Bahá'u'lláh predicted a dramatic loss of power by ecclesiastical institutions: "O concourse of divines! Ye shall not henceforward behold yourselves possessed of any power, inasmuch as We have seized it from you, and destined it for such as have believed in God . . ." (PDC 81) Ecclesiastical hierarchies which, in the trappings of state religion, once enjoyed financial and political ties to great nations, have since lost their patronage. Throughout most of this century, a growing crisis of confidence in organized religion has eroded not only its worldly dominance, but its moral authority, while the baneful effects of materialism and secular humanism have invaded every cranny of modern life.

In particular, Bahá'u'lláh wrote to Pope Pius IX, advising him of God's preference that he voluntarily "Abandon thy kingdom unto the kings . . ." (PDC 32) Had he heeded this counsel, published in 1869, the pontiff would have spared himself the anguish of losing Italy the following year to conquest by King Victor Emmanuel.

PROPHECY 11: *The collapse of the Muslim Caliphate.*
The Báb, Bahá'u'lláh's forerunner, had explicitly predicted that God's wrath would descend upon the Caliphate with "the most afflictive torment . . . the most dire and exemplary punishment" (GPB 231). Bahá'u'lláh Himself confirmed this prophecy by alluding to the downfall of Islam's "mighty throne" as a foregone conclusion (GPB 231). When the Sultanate was abolished after World War I, the former sultan, Muhammad VI, continued for several more years to retain his title as Caliph. This awkward arrangement, however, displeased the rulers of the new Turkish republic, who in 1924 dissolved and dissociated themselves from the age-old institution. The ex-Caliph fled ignominiously, and the Muslim world's frantic efforts to create a new Caliphate all collapsed in partisan bickering.

The Movement of the Left

PROPHECY 12: *The spread of communism, the "Movement of the Left",*
and its rise to world power.
PROPHECY 13: *The catastrophic decline of that same movement, triggered*
by the collapse of its egalitarian economy.
Communism is denounced in the Bahá'í teachings as one of three "false gods" at whose altars modern nations have worshipped (PDC 113). (The other two are racialism and nationalism.) Shortly after the Bolshevik Revolu-

tion of 1917 'Abdu'l-Bahá, speaking of "Movements, newly-born and worldwide in their range", stated: "The Movement of the Left will acquire great importance. Its influence will spread" (WOB 30). Leftist ideology, embodied in a variety of communist and socialist uprisings, did indeed gain worldwide momentum hardly any of 'Abdu'l-Bahá's contemporaries could have visualized. The resulting Cold War polarized and paralyzed the world for decades, holding every human being hostage to a hair-trigger nuclear standoff. Nevertheless, the basic economic premise of communism was described in the Bahá'í teachings as certain to "end in disorderliness, in chaos, in disorganization of the means of existence, and in universal disappointment", destroying the order of the community (SAQ 278). The truth of this prophecy became evident in the late 1980s and early 1990s as the worldwide collapse of communism reduced its mighty empire to a wasteland of splintered and squabbling republics.

The Jews: Homeland and Holocaust

PROPHECY 14: *The rise of Israel as a Jewish homeland.*
PROPHECY 15: *The persecution of Jews on the European continent (the Nazi Holocaust).*

Both Bahá'u'lláh and 'Abdu'l-Bahá clearly anticipated the fulfilment, in our own time, of Old Testament promises concerning the regathering of Jews in the Holy Land (SAQ 65-66). These expectations have been largely vindicated by the establishment and continuing consolidation of the State of Israel. The Bahá'í outlook was tempered, however, by a dire warning. Decades before the Nazi Holocaust 'Abdu'l-Bahá pleaded with Jewish audiences to guard against a renewed outbreak of savage persecution on the European continent (PUP 414).

America's Racial Upheavals

PROPHECY 16: *America's violent racial struggles.*

Long before most Americans recognized either the injustice or the danger of their country's "race problem", the Bahá'í teachings sounded a trumpet-call for action to bridge black-white differences (ADJ 33, BWF 359). 'Abdu'l-Bahá plainly stated in 1912 that without a prompt change of heart, America would lose credibility and moral authority throughout the globe, eventually finding its own streets red with blood (*Star of the West*, vol. XXII, p. 121; CF 126). Most white Americans of that era would have found such warnings extravagant, if not incomprehensible. Yet they have since been justified by decades of racial strife, bloodshed, and polarization.

BAHÁ'U'LLÁH AND HIS FAITH

A number of Bahá'u'lláh's prophecies specifically described future developments in the religion of which He was the Head and Founder.

Bahá'u'lláh's Release from Prison

PROPHECY 17: *Bahá'u'lláh's release from the prison of 'Akká and the pitching of His tent on Mount Carmel.*

En route to the maximum-security penal colony of 'Akká, Bahá'u'lláh – sentenced to life without appeal or parole – confidently promised that He would leave the prison, pitch His tent on Mount Carmel and transform His sufferings into "the outpourings of a supreme mercy" (PDC 42, AB 39). Against all odds, and through circumstances so miraculous as to defy belief, He did precisely that.

The House of Bahá'u'lláh

PROPHECY 18: *The seizure and desecration of the House of Bahá'u'-lláh in Baghdad.*

Bahá'u'lláh foretold that the house He occupied while living in Baghdad (and which He later ordained as a center of pilgrimage for Bahá'ís) would one day be "abased" by enemies of the Faith, that the "veil of [its] sanctity" would be "rent asunder" by them in such manner as to "cause tears to flow from every discerning eye" (G 114-115). Around the time of 'Abdu'l-Bahá's passing, Shí'ih Muslims in Baghdad – seemingly intent on vindicating Bahá'u'lláh's prediction – occupied the building, expelled its Bahá'í owners and defied a later high court ruling unanimously denouncing the seizure as illegal. Although Bahá'ís are certain they will one day regain their rightful property, they have now been barred from this sacred and historic site for more than ninety years.

Bahá'í Unity

PROPHECY 19: *The failure of all attempts to create schism within the Bahá'í Faith.*

Almost every world faith has repeatedly divided and subdivided into sects, denominations, factions and splinter groups, all competing for the allegiance of believers. Bahá'u'lláh took steps to protect the Bahá'í Faith from this divisive tendency; and He promised that it would, as a result, remain both administratively and spiritually unified for all time (GPB 99 & 326, WOB 23 & 109). The strength of this amazing prophecy has been tested, time and again, by cunning internal enemies eager to advance their own agendas. Not one of the offshoots they have devised, however ingeniously, has ever flourished or attracted a significant following. Meanwhile, Bahá'u'lláh's Cause, structured as He Himself intended, has spread throughout the earth, becoming (according to non-Bahá'í authorities) the most widespread religion after Christianity and in all likelihood the most diverse organized body on the planet.

SCIENTIFIC PROPHECIES

Some of the most important scientific and technical developments of the present age were announced beforehand in the Bahá'í sacred writings.

The Knowledge Explosion

PROPHECY 20: *The explosive acceleration of scientific and technological progress.*

Bahá'u'lláh appeared in a world where technical progress, though uneven, had always been relatively slow. Generations before Him had lived and died knowing that their great-grandchildren would be born into a world little more advanced than their own. The prophecies of Bahá'u'lláh made it clear that that world had ended; that in the new heavens and new earth of His revelation, scientific knowledge and invention would dart forward with jackrabbit speed (see Taherzadeh, *Revelation*, vol. III, p. 137). Beginning at once, He said, humanity would "behold things of which ye have never heard before" including "the knowledge of the most marvelous sciences" (G 141-2) – hitherto unimaginable discoveries that would shrink the globe to a veritable village. These advances (though exposing humankind to catastrophic danger) would provide a material framework for the infinitely more glorious spiritual revolution to follow, a revolution destined to usher in the millennial paradise promised in scriptures of old.

Nuclear Terror

PROPHECY 21: *The development of nuclear weapons.*

Shortly before His ascension in 1892, Bahá'u'lláh warned that the arms race, if not halted, could lead to "strange and astonishing" weapons of unthinkable horror: "These things are capable of changing the whole atmosphere of the earth and their contamination would prove lethal." (TB 69) These measured words must have sounded, to His generation, like the ravings of a madman. 'Abdu'l-Bahá in 1911 advised a Japanese diplomat to pray that this "stupendous force, as yet, happily, undiscovered by man . . . be not discovered until spiritual civilization shall dominate the human mind".

In the hands of unredeemed men, He added, "this power would be able to destroy the whole earth" (*Chosen Highway* 184). The 1945 atomic bombing of Hiroshima and Nagasaki announced to the world that Bahá'u'lláh and His successor knew whereof they spoke.

Copper into Gold

PROPHECY 22: *The achievement of transmutation of elements, the age-old alchemist's dream.*

PROPHECY 23: *Dire peril for all humanity as a result of that achievement.*

Western scientists of Bahá'u'lláh's day believed that transmutation – the changing of one chemical element into another – was theoretically impossible. Bahá'u'lláh explained that they were mistaken. He wrote that copper (for example) can become gold or vice versa: "Every mineral can be made to acquire the density, form and substance of each and every other mineral." (G 197-198) Only decades later did physicists realize that elemental atoms are not, as they once thought, the smallest irreducible building blocks of matter. Atoms are composed of still smaller particles that can be separated and recombined, the result being that any element can indeed change into any other. Unfortunately, transmutation (as Bahá'u'lláh also foresaw) is far from an unmixed blessing (see Taherzadeh, *Revelation*, vol. II, p. 268). It has opened the door to global holocaust by virtue of its link with nuclear explosive technology.

The Evolution of Elements

PROPHECY 24: *The discovery that complex elements evolve in nature from simpler ones.*

The Bahá'í teachings state that "in the beginning matter was one", giving rise to elements which became differentiated only "after a very long time" into their present complex forms (SAQ 181). This teaching seemed, at the time, irreconcilable with known facts; but its truth became apparent by the middle of the twentieth century. Physicists now realize that all matter begins as hydrogen gas which, collecting slowly in suns and stars, cooks under enormous pressure for thousands of millions of years. The resulting nuclear reactions combine the original atoms of hydrogen into heavier and ever-more-complex elements. These elements eventually render the star unstable, triggering (if it is sufficiently massive) a "supernova" explosion which welds vast quantities of starstuff into still heavier elements and flings them into space as gas. The constant repetition of this process throughout the universe provides the raw material for suns and planets such as our own.

51

Stars and Planets

PROPHECY 25: *The recognition of planets as a necessary by-product of star formation.*

Another scientific mystery in Bahá'u'lláh's day was whether stars other than our own sun have planets. Bahá'u'lláh Himself was explicit: "Every fixed star", He wrote, "hath its own planets . . ." (G 163) (The traditional term "fixed star" refers to self-luminous stellar bodies like our own sun, in contrast to planets that once were called "wandering stars".) Throughout most of the 20th century astronomers insisted that planets cannot occur naturally but only as a result of some freak catastrophe such as a near-collision between stars. Not until the early 1970s did new mathematical models show that the rotation of a star necessarily spins off a disk of matter, forming rings that coalesce into orbiting bodies. According to current knowledge, then, every normal star will at some point sire planets as part of its natural life-cycle.

Railroads to Heaven

PROPHECY 26: *Space travel.*

The Bahá'í teachings specifically predict space travel and describe some of its characteristics and future accomplishments. Speaking in Paris in 1913, 'Abdu'l-Bahá stated that the time had come to direct efforts towards reaching other planets (AB 377). Elsewhere He envisioned vehicles traveling with "the rapidity of rising lightning" from the earth to the heavens and even "from the globe of the earth to the globe of the sun" (TAB 32). Today's reusable shuttle, the solar probe Ulysses, and other space ventures have fulfilled every word of these predictions.

Transmission of Cancer

PROPHECY 27: *The realization that some forms of cancer are communicable.*

'Abdu'l-Bahá counted cancer among "bodily diseases" which (in at least some forms and to some extent) are communicable among human beings (LG 183). This statement, when published in 1921, defied established medical opinion. In recent years, however, new evidence has linked some cancers of the reproductive system to human papilloma virus, an infection authorities believe can be sexually transmitted. (This is not true of most – much less all – malignancies; and none, so far as we now know, are spread by casual contact.)

The Missing "Missing Link"

PROPHECY 28: *Failure to find evidence for a "missing link" between man and ape.*

'Abdu'l-Bahá stated flatly in 1912 that no anthropologist or palae-ontologist would ever unearth fossil proof for the so-called "missing link" – the purported common ancestor between human beings and modern apes (PUP 358-359). His statement, though debunked for decades by skeptics, has held up to a century of intense archeological scrutiny. The only skeletal specimen ever seriously touted as likely to overturn it was the notorious "Piltdown Man", announced the very year 'Abdu'l-Bahá made His prediction. More than forty years later, Piltdown Man was exposed as a clever hoax.

The Missing Ether

PROPHECY 29: *The nonexistence of a mechanical ether (the supposed light-carrying medium posited by classical physics) and its redefinition as an abstract reality.*

Physicists of the nineteenth and early twentieth centuries believed in an undetectable substance called ether – one that supposedly pervaded all space, defining its extent and acting as a medium for light and other electromagnetic waveforms. 'Abdu'l-Bahá challenged this concept, denying that ether has any objective physical existence. It should be regarded – He said – rather as an intellectual abstraction (SAQ 83-84). This position was later vindicated by Einstein as a key insight of his theory of relativity. The crude, mechanical ether of yesteryear is replaced in modern theory by a quasi-mathematical framework physicists call the "fabric" of the space-time continuum. Although most scientists (with notable exceptions such as Einstein, Jeans and Eddington) decline to use the old-fashioned name, this radically redefined ether is an entity whose characteristics precisely match those affirmed by 'Abdu'l-Bahá.

The Collapse of Mechanical Models

PROPHECY 30: *The breakdown of mechanical models (literal images) as a basis for understanding the physical world.*

Classical physics had relied for centuries on mechanical models as a supposedly all-sufficient basis for understanding the physical world. (A mechanical model is an image or replica corresponding in some objective way – not merely a metaphorical way – to the thing it represents.) 'Abdu'l-

53

Bahá stated forcefully that "nature . . . in its essence" is utterly incompatible with mechanical models. Its deepest building blocks can no more be expressed by objective description than can such abstractions as "love" or "truth" (SAQ 84). Such assertions were, at that time, even more daring and radical than 'Abdu'l-Bahá's rejection of a material ether. Yet His insights were fully validated, more than fifteen years later, by the development of quantum mechanics – the mathematical description of subatomic particles and their behavior. The resulting collapse of mechanical models lies at the very heart of the revolution in physics which, in this century, has shaken the world, transformed every aspect of modern life, and (in the words of Sir James Jeans) made the universe appear "more like a great thought than like a great machine".

*****

These predictions – and the circumstances by which each one was dramatically fulfilled – are fully documented in *The Challenge of Bahá'u'lláh* and *He Cometh with Clouds*. (Both books are by Gary L. Matthews and available from George Ronald, Publisher.) Most of these prophecies pertain to specific events within an identifiable time frame. Any or all could have turned out differently in such a way as to cast doubt upon Bahá'u'lláh's claim. Most, when first written or uttered, defied conventional wisdom. Yet not one prophecy proved to be in error. Each one has "come to pass on this earth" just as Bahá'u'lláh promised, often in spectacular ways and sometimes at the last possible moment.

Other prophecies of Bahá'u'lláh and 'Abdu'l-Bahá seem intimately related to ongoing developments taking place in the world today. These prophecies foretold, among other things, that a worldwide tide of oppression would be followed by a renaissance of liberty, leading ultimately to "unity in freedom"; that a "new world order" would emerge in which all nations, driven by "imperative necessity", would collectively resist aggression by any recalcitrant member; that these and other trends would lead ultimately to "the unity of nations – a unity which in this century will be firmly established, causing all the peoples of the world to regard themselves as citizens of one common fatherland"; the cataclysmic "rolling up" of the "present-day Order" as a prelude to world peace; the preponderating role to be played by America in the forging of that peace; the emergence of the Bahá'í Faith from obscurity and, as a temporary consequence, its repression in various parts of the world. While none of the prophecies in this latter category are as yet completely fulfilled, all are at least partially fulfilled; and events are moving swiftly in the directions they indicate.

The plain fact is that 'Abdu'l-Bahá's confident assertion, uttered more than a full and awesomely turbulent century ago, today rings truer than ever:

"... all that was recorded in the Tablets to the Kings is being fulfilled: if from the year A.D. 1870 we compare the events that have occurred, we will find everything that has happened has appeared as predicted; only a few remain which will afterward become manifested." (SAQ 33-4)

Chapter Five
THE OBJECT OF ALL KNOWLEDGE

We have decreed, O people, that the highest and last end of all learning be the recognition of Him Who is the Object of all knowledge; and yet, behold how ye have allowed your learning to shut you out, as by a veil, from Him Who is the Dayspring of this Light. . . .

—*Bahá'u'lláh*

Knowledge is a light which God casteth into the heart of whomsoever He willeth.

—*Muḥammad*

THE HISTORICAL PREDICTIONS and scientific disclosures we have been considering can help us decide whether Bahá'u'lláh displayed knowledge not readily available to Him through normal human channels. However, there also are other avenues by which we can test the nature and extent of His knowledge. These, like the ones we have already explored, have a distinct bearing on the broader question of His identity and the validity of His claim to be the bearer of a divine message.

The term "Manifestation of God," as defined by Bahá'u'lláh, obviously means much more than an inspired predictor of future events. It signifies, among other things, a world educator guided by God to deliver spiritual and social principles for a new civilization and endowed by Him with "a divine power to put them into effect." ('Abdu'l-Bahá, PUP 250) As 'Abdu'l-Bahá frequently remarked, the proof of an educator lies not in miraculous displays but in his power to educate. The teachings of a Divine Manifestation must both anticipate the needs of the age to come and help shape that age. This requires knowledge of the future, but it requires a vast amount of other knowledge as well.

Bahá'u'lláh stipulates, moreover, that the knowledge of a Manifestation is *innate*. Being a divine gift, it is inborn, intuitive – not acquired through study or reflection. To show that someone's knowledge was the product of ordinary human learning would therefore be to show that that person was not, in the Bahá'í sense, a Manifestation of God. This would be true no matter how brilliant or well-read the individual in question happened to be.

These considerations open several promising lines of inquiry. How extensive was Bahá'u'lláh's knowledge? Did He undergo schooling or engage in research? Were His insights radically beyond the established learning of His day? Did He display skills or abilities that no amount of training could confer? Most important, was His knowledge really comprehensive enough to fit Him for the mission He undertook – the launching of a new and higher civilization?

The answers to such questions ought to shed considerable light on the authenticity of Bahá'u'lláh's inspiration. Should the answers prove strongly consistent with His claim, they would greatly strengthen the probability that it is true. These matters are of course fraught with value judgments that reasonable people may well make differently. Nevertheless, the facts of Bahá'u'lláh's life are sufficiently well documented that any serious inquirer can proceed with considerable confidence. For anyone seeking to assess the validity of the Bahá'í revelation, these questions bear directly on our central issue: *Who was Bahá'u'lláh?*

Bahá'u'lláh's Background

Bahá'u'lláh's native Persia was a land of rich culture and startling contrasts. It was the remnant of an ancient civilization that, at its height, had dominated most of the civilized world. In Old Testament days, Zoroastrian Persia had ruled an empire stretching from "the inner confines of India and China to the farthermost reaches of Yemen and Ethiopia." ('Abdu'l-Baha, SDC 7) During her long and glamorous history, Persia produced kings such as Cyrus and Darius; poets such as Ḥáfiz, Rúmí, Sa'dí and 'Umar Khayyám; and artisans who dazzled the world with unrivaled carpets, steel blades, pottery and other handiwork. "This fairest of lands," writes 'Abdu'l-Bahá, "was once a lamp, streaming with the rays of Divine knowledge, of science and art, of nobility and high achievement, of wisdom and valor." (ibid. 9)

By the eighteenth and nineteenth centuries, however, Persia had sunk into an appalling state of backwardness and decay. It had become, in the words of Sir Valentine Chirol, "a country gangrened with corruption and atrophied with indifferentism." (Chirol, *The Middle Eastern Question* 120, quoted in *Appreciations* 21) Persia's people – rich and poor, learned and illiterate – were drowning in superstition and fanaticism. The country was a feudal autocracy whose rulers wielded iron control over a docile and apathetic populace. Its Muslim priesthood, vested with enormous political power, maintained sway over both rulers and populace by regularly whipping both into an emotional frenzy. Women were regarded as little more than livestock, foreigners and religious minorities as accursed heathen, and liberal ideas generally as satanic. Criminals were tortured to death in carnival-like public celebrations, the word "criminal" being loosely construed to mean anyone who happened to displease the local priest or governor. Bribery was the indispensable lubricant of every transaction, public or private.

This was the environment of Bahá'u'lláh's formative years – the only one He knew prior to assuming His prophetic ministry. The suffocating effects of this benighted social atmosphere pervaded every department of life, including education. Most Persians were entirely uneducated, and even the upper classes (which included the nobility, government officials and well-to-do merchants) seldom aspired to anything beyond functional literacy. Male children of privileged families customarily received a few years of home tutoring in reading and writing, with emphasis on the Qur'án, Persian religious poetry, and ornate penmanship. Despite its artistic flavor, such training was rudimentary, far greater importance being attached to marksmanship, swordplay, horseback riding and other physical skills. With rare exceptions, formal schooling was reserved for the professional clergy, whose members were accepted without question as the divinely intended custodians of knowledge. These men, fiercely protective of their elite status, regarded both the nobility and the peasantry as inferior beings unfit for higher learning.

Bahá'u'lláh, being the child of a prominent government official, received the same sketchy tutoring as others of His high rank. By the standards of His own society, He was literate but not learned. At no time did He attend school or devote Himself to scholarly pursuits. This very lack of academic grounding soon excited comment as He acquired a reputation for unusual knowledge and insight. As a young man, He repeatedly astounded the divines by unraveling mysteries that had defied their collective ingenuity. Both before and after He became known as the head of the Bahá'í movement, His erudition won the respect of outstanding scholars and men of letters throughout the Middle East, including many who did not accept Him as divinely inspired. Experts in diverse fields sought and received His help in solving problems peculiar to their own specialties, and even His enemies were wont to call Him "the renowned Bahá'u'lláh." His voluminous letters, addressed to persons from a wide assortment of ethnic and religious communities, show intimate familiarity with the diverse scriptural, historical, and literary traditions of those individuals.

That an unschooled individual should gain such preeminence among the foremost scholars and savants of His time is surely without precedent.

We cannot, of course, afford to rely blindly on the judgment of Bahá'u'lláh's admiring contemporaries any more than we would rely blindly on those who denounced Him as a subversive madman. Fortunately, most of His original writings have been preserved; a comprehensive and representative selection of these has been translated into English and many other languages, and more translations are appearing all the time. Bahá'u'lláh did not restrict these writings to such stereotypically "religious" topics as metaphysics and character development. He revealed divine principles governing issues in law, international relations, arms control, political administration, education, group dynamics, economics, health, psychology, medicine and science, to name just a few. These writings, along with the large and growing body of scholarly literature they have evoked, make it fairly easy for any thoughtful reader to assess Bahá'u'lláh's contributions objectively. Many distinguished people, familiar with these contributions in their respective fields yet themselves not Bahá'ís, have praised His work in terms scarcely less glowing than those of His nineteenth-century admirers.

Vast erudition is not necessarily a token of divine inspiration. We do not regard men such as Aristotle, Leonardo da Vinci, Isaac Newton, or Albert Einstein as bearers of revealed truth. The reason is that we can, by studying their lives, trace their gradual acquisition of knowledge through years of schooling and research. Westerners often approach the study of Bahá'u'lláh with the preconception that He can be explained in the same way – that His was a brilliant and creative mind blossoming under the benign influence of a cosmopolitan environment, advanced education, and contact with other similarly gifted individuals. His brilliance and creativity are not, of course, in doubt; but every other element of this explanation is false. Bahá'u'lláh grew to adulthood in an atmosphere of extreme prejudice, fanaticism, superstition, and ignorance. The limited education He received offered nothing to counteract the pernicious influence of His early conditioning or to explain the phenomenal knowledge and vision He displayed. We may – indeed we must – say He rose above the limitations of His environment. We cannot explain Him as its product.

Recognizing this fact, we may suspect that Bahá'u'lláh was simply a self-taught prodigy. Living in the modern West, we are accustomed to believing that any sufficiently motivated person can acquire an education by voracious reading. However, matters were not so simple in nineteenth-century Persia. Bahá'u'lláh was, from His earliest youth, a well-known, highly visible figure at a time when it was unthinkable for a man of his station to pursue higher learning. Public libraries were unknown. Books – often hand-copied – were rare and exorbitantly expensive. Scholarly reference libraries were confined to Muslim theological universities, where they were haunted by the clergy – men who would have bristled at the thought of a "lesser mortal" invading their sacred turf. Bahá'u'lláh might have found a way to gain access to a university library, or He might (by spending a large chunk of the family fortune) have built up a useful private collection. But He could not have carried out either project, much less devoted years of His life to personal research, without attracting widespread attention. So brazen an affront to the rigid customs of Persian society would have raised eyebrows and aroused indignation throughout much of the country.

The fact that Bahá'u'lláh did none of these things is one of the strongest points of agreement between His supporters and His avowed enemies. When He advanced His claim to be a Manifestation of God, His adversaries – missing the point altogether – countered by stressing His entire lack of higher education. Many found it impossible to believe that God might choose as His instrument of revelation someone who had never earned a degree in theology. Bahá'u'lláh acknowledged their protests:

> "Lay not aside the fear of God, O ye the learned of the world, and judge fairly the cause of this unlettered One. . . .
> "Certain ones among both commoners and nobles have objected that this wronged One is neither a member of the ecclesiastical order nor a descendant of the Prophet. Say: O ye that claim to be just! Reflect a little while, and ye shall recognize how infinitely exalted is His present state above the station ye claim He should possess. The Will of the Almighty hath decreed that out of a house wholly devoid of all that the divines, the doctors, the sages and scholars commonly possess His Cause shall proceed and be made manifest." (G 98-9)

His Tablet to the sháh states:

> ". . . the breezes of the All-Glorious were wafted over Me, and taught me the knowledge of all that hath been. . . . The learning current amongst men I studied not; their schools I entered not. Ask of the city wherein I dwelt, that thou mayest be well assured that I am not of them who speak falsely." (ESW 39)

Still, a fact is one thing, its interpretation quite another. There is no serious doubt that Bahá'u'lláh was "unlettered" (as He and His detractors insisted). A skeptic may naturally wonder, however, whether His supposedly innate knowledge has been exaggerated. We can always construct elaborate scenarios purporting to show how Bahá'u'lláh might have acquired the necessary training in secrecy. However unwarranted or farfetched such ideas may be, many people understandably will find them more plausible than the idea of divine revelation. It would therefore be helpful if we could identify

61

specific features of Bahá'u'lláh's knowledge that cannot easily be dismissed as overblown or explained away as the result of clandestine study. As it happens, there are several such features. One of them we have already explored in detail – namely, the occurrence in Bahá'u'lláh's writings of many daring but accurate predictions. However, there are at least three other factors that, given His situation, weigh heavily against any effort to equate His knowledge with ordinary human learning. These are (1) the farsightedness of Bahá'u'lláh's social principles, (2) His phenomenal mastery of Arabic, and (3) the speed and spontaneity with which He composed His writings. Let us examine each of these factors more closely.

Farsightedness

The characteristic I call "farsightedness" refers to the way Bahá'u'lláh's teachings have consistently proved to be ahead of their time. A century and more after His passing – a period during which the world has changed more than in all previous recorded history – His writings remain astoundingly modern in tone, outlook, and substance. This modernity becomes more striking each year as the world develops along lines that render His teachings ever more suitable to its needs. Bahá'u'lláh did not write only about the world in which He lived. He also wrote, explicitly and with exceptional insight, about the world in which we live today – a twenty-first century global village. In so doing He gave humanity its *first comprehensive inventory* of the principles now generally held to be on the cutting edge of social advancement. His proposals have set the agenda for all the great upheavals and reform struggles that have raged ever since.

The result of this evolutionary process has been described by George Townshend in the following words:

"The humanitarian and spiritual principles enunciated decades ago in the darkest East by Bahá'u'lláh and molded by Him into a coherent scheme are one after the other being taken by a world unconscious of their source as the marks of progressive civilization." (DB, Introduction xxxvi)

Commenting on the same phenomenon, Townshend again writes:

"Slowly the veil lifts from the future. Along whatever road thoughtful men look out they see before them some guiding truth, some leading principle, which Bahá'u'lláh gave long ago and which men rejected." (GPB, Introduction ix.)

THE OBJECT OF ALL KNOWLEDGE

This gradual and largely unconscious adoption of Bahá'í ideals as symbols of enlightened modernism has become the single most pervasive trend of our time. Examples abound; an especially revealing one occurred in April 1963, the month when Bahá'ís celebrated the centenary of Bahá'u'lláh's formal declaration of His mission.

In that very month, Pope John XXIII issued his last pastoral letter, the encyclical *Pacem in Terris* (Peace on Earth). This brilliant document – a summary of the prerequisites for peace and progress in the decades ahead – evoked worldwide praise from non-Catholics and Catholics alike. Pope John did not claim originality for any of his points. He presented them simply as a fusion and synthesis of the best in contemporary thought, weaving them into a single package in order to bring them to the forefront of public discussion. The principles were: (1) creation of a world community; (2) independent investigation of truth; (3) universal education; (4) equality of men and women; (5) abolition of prejudice; (6) recognition of the oneness of God; (7) the reconciliation of science and religion; (8) world disarmament; (9) a spiritual approach to economics; and (10) loyalty to government. Also included was a warning on the dangers of atomic energy. (For detailed citations from "Pacem in Terris," correlating its highlights with those of Bahá'í scripture, see Ugo Giachery, "One God, One Truth, One People," *The Bahá'í World,* vol. XV, pp. 612-19.)

Every one of these points is a recurring theme of Bahá'u'lláh's writings.* With the exception of His own warning on atomic energy (circa 1890), they all are major planks of the peace program He drafted in the late 1860s and early 1870s, and which He in that same period called to the attention of world leaders including Pope Pius IX. Bahá'u'lláh, unlike Pope John, gave detailed guidance on translating these matters from theory into practice. By the time the Pope announced the principles, they already had become familiar to enlightened men and women everywhere. Bahá'u'lláh, however, announced them at a time when they were largely unknown both to leaders of thought

---

*There is no "official" list of Bahá'í principles. Bahá'u'lláh's writings seldom contain descriptive headings; they cover thousands of topics and defy easy categorization. To indicate the spirit of His teachings, however, Bahá'í writers generally list eight to twelve thematic ideas, rewording or rearranging them slightly to suit the context. Two important Bahá'í principles are missing from *Pacem in Terris* – the essential unity of all religions and the adoption of a universal auxiliary language. Otherwise, its main points correspond closely to the familiar principles listed and described in hundreds of Bahá'í publications since the Faith's beginning.

and to the public, their feasibility had not been seriously explored in any part of the world, and their interconnectedness as peace prerequisites was quite unheard of.

A Bahá'í might naturally interpret Bahá'u'lláh's advanced outlook as simply one more aspect of His ability to see the future – an ability attested by the review of prophecies in previous chapters. However, I have chosen not to discuss it under that heading because it seems to me to involve much more than mere predictive power. We can easily imagine a psychic who is able to predict the future with pinpoint accuracy (right down to, say, stock market fluctuations) but unable to produce anything of lasting spiritual or social value. Bahá'u'lláh clearly was much more than this. It is His analysis of policy questions, as distinct from mere predictions or statements of fact, that most powerfully demonstrates His grasp of modern realities.

However we interpret His modernity, it clearly betokens a knowledge far ahead of anything He might have learned or deduced from any course of study available in His lifetime. We cannot realistically say that Bahá'u'lláh "merely" displayed an unusual gift for extrapolating future trends from existing conditions. Modern sociologists consider it humanly impossible – even with the aid of up-to-the-minute research libraries, electronic databanks, computer simulations, and the like – to project social trends more than a few years into the future. Every attempt at scientific forecasting of social changes has been a dismal failure. Even if we suppose Bahá'u'lláh might somehow have succeeded where today's science fails, such a feat would have required an extraordinary amount of raw data. The requisite information for such far-reaching deductions certainly was not to be found in nineteenth-century Middle Eastern literature. Whether it was available in the West is doubtful but entirely moot: Bahá'u'lláh had no access to Western literature and no contact, save for one brief visit in the closing days of His life, with any Western scholar.

We must also remember that the nineteenth century produced many outstanding intellectuals and visionaries who studied in the best universities, worked in the best libraries, and shared ideas and insights with one another. Not one of these thinkers, in the East or the West, even came close to matching Bahá'u'lláh's vision. He alone, with none of their advantages, produced the writings that have best stood the test of time – the only writings that each year become more relevant to world events, rather than less, and the only ones conspicuously free of the narrow outlook, naive misconceptions, and outright superstition that plagued the thought of His day. Surely these considerations challenge us to weigh seriously Bahá'u'-lláh's own explanation: "This thing is not from Me, but from One Who is Almighty and All-Knowing." (PDC 40)

Bahá'u'lláh's Use of Arabic

Bahá'u'lláh's insight into the problems and conditions of a future age undoubtedly is impressive. As evidence of inspired knowledge, however, it is admittedly circumstantial. If nothing else, we can always chalk it up to a series of fantastically lucky guesses. Can we point to some specific, highly technical body of knowledge that Bahá'u'lláh demonstrably mastered without study – a subject that normally cannot be acquired without years of training? Such a subject is not hard to find. It is the Arabic written language. 'Abdu'l-Bahá, discussing proofs of inspiration, cites Bahá'u'lláh's virtuosity with classical Arabic as a clear example of innate knowledge:

> *"Bahá'u'lláh had never studied Arabic; He had not had a tutor or teacher, nor had He entered a school. Nevertheless, the eloquence and elegance of His blessed expositions in Arabic, as well as His Arabic writings, caused astonishment and stupefaction to the most accomplished Arabic scholars, and all recognized and declared that He was incomparable and unequaled."* (SAQ 34)

This point deserves careful consideration. One of the first things a student of the Bahá'í Faith learns is that Bahá'u'lláh wrote both in Persian and in Arabic. This fact, in itself, hardly seems surprising: Millions of people are bilingual, with or without formal training. For an uninformed Westerner, there is a natural tendency to assume that Persian and Arabic probably are similar languages, widely used by Bahá'u'lláh's countrymen, from whom He might have acquired both by simple exposure. Such an assumption, however, turns out to be flawed in two key respects.

First, Persian and Arabic do not especially resemble one another. They have similar alphabets, to be sure (Persian has four extra letters), and there has been some mutual influence. This derives in part from the fact that they are spoken in adjacent countries. A more fundamental reason is that Islam, the prevailing religion of Persia, reveres as its holy book the Qur'án, which was originally revealed in Arabic. But the differences are profound, and they far outweigh any cosmetic similarities. The two do not even belong to the same family of languages: Arabic is Semitic while Persian is Indo-European.

Second, Arabic is not widely used or spoken in Persia; nor was it so used or spoken in Bahá'u'lláh's lifetime. Neither the nobility nor the peasantry, as a rule, knew anything of the language. The one class for which knowledge of Arabic was considered important was the Islamic clergy, who used it in their study of the Qur'án. These Muslim divines labored for years to master the subtleties of Arabic grammar and vocabulary, as well as its complex literary conventions. Most of them regarded no treatise as worthy of attention unless it was written in Arabic, and they tended to pepper their sermons and discourses with complex Arabic expressions that few if any members of their congregations could fathom.

It is certainly possible to acquire a working knowledge of conversational Arabic through association with persons who speak it. This is how all children first learn their native tongues. There is, however, a peculiarity of Arabic that takes on extreme importance in this connection: "In Arabic, distinction should be made between the written, or classical form, and the spoken, or colloquial." (Phillip K. Hitti, "Arab Civilization," *Encyclopedia Americana,* 1990, vol. II, p. 152) Ordinary spoken Arabic takes the form of various local dialects or vernaculars, which are used in everyday commerce but rarely written. None of these has much in common with any of the others. In contrast, written Arabic (also known as "standard" or "formal" Arabic) is the same throughout the Arabic-speaking world. It is therefore used for literary and technical communication as well as for diplomatic correspondence. It is, however, markedly different from any of the standard dialects in its vocabulary, its grammar, its syntax, and its stylistic requirements.* Simply put, written and conversational Arabic differ enough to constitute, for all practical purposes, different languages.

This radical distinction between the written and spoken word has consequences that might seem odd to an English-speaking individual. Much Arabic fiction, for instance, gives the impression of being written in two languages, the classical for narrative and a local vernacular for dialogue. Other fiction uses the classical form throughout, producing dialogue with little resemblance to actual speech anywhere, and a few works use the vernacular only. We are accustomed to the idea that anyone who speaks excellent English and who knows script well enough to transcribe that English word for word can write excellent English as well. Indeed, the best advice an English teacher can give a student is "Speak correctly, and write the way you speak." But this would be terrible advice for a student of Arabic! One might learn to converse in fluent or even eloquent Arabic and learn in addition to copy one's speech onto paper verbatim. Yet doing so would not enable anyone to write Arabic that is correct or even necessarily comprehensible. One would remain, in every way that matters, quite illiterate.

---

*Though rarely used in face-to-face communication, the spoken form of classical Arabic is employed on certain formal occasions and, today, is used increasingly on Arabic radio.

Learning to write adequately – not brilliantly, just adequately – in Arabic requires years of disciplined instruction. A. F. L. Beeston, author of *The Arabic Language Today*, states flatly that the classical Arabic used for writing and formal speech "must be learned in school." (Beeston, "Arabic Language," *Academic American Encyclopedia*, 1989, vol. II, p. 100) The details of the language are subtle, intricate, and arbitrary. They are acquired through painstaking drill and memorization. A structured training program administered by a competent instructor is generally deemed indispensable. With this sort of grounding, one may become passably literate.

Even more difficult, by a whole order of magnitude, is the specialized literary Arabic used in Muslim religious writing. "In this latter case," says *Collier's Encyclopedia*, "the knowledge of Arabic is restricted to the learned." (G. L. Della Vida, "Arabic Language," *Collier's*, 1990, vol. II, p. 393) This form presents technical challenges so imposing as to daunt any but the most accomplished experts. Native Arabic-speaking scholars, steeped from childhood in the richness and beauty of the language, intimately familiar with its culture and traditions, can and do spend lifetimes augmenting their knowledge of this seemingly infinite subject.

Bahá'u'lláh, as stated above, had no training in Arabic and no experience that might have equipped Him to deal with its complex literary formalities. However, from the earliest beginnings of His forty-year prophetic ministry, He wrote interchangeably in Persian and Arabic, proving Himself equally adept in both languages. His Arabic compositions – some in prose, others in poetry – are unrivaled whether from the standpoint of literary beauty or technical proficiency. Though He often broke with convention, preferring to originate His own distinctive styles, His command of established patterns was complete. Time and again He demonstrated His ability to work in any classical or traditional form, adhering strictly to its most rigorous requirements.

Many of Bahá'u'lláh's writings, both Persian and Arabic, are available in English translation. Through these (particularly the superb renderings of Shoghi Effendi) one may obtain a glimpse of the towering eloquence and beauty of His composition and the diversity of styles at His command. Sadly, it is a glimpse and nothing more: According to all competent testimony, the originals are in every respect incomparably superior to the translations. Shoghi Effendi describes one of his own finest translations as "one more attempt . . . in language however inadequate" to "assist others in their efforts to approach what must always be regarded as the unattainable goal – a befitting rendering of Bahá'u'lláh's matchless utterance." (KI, foreword vii) Some of Bahá'u'lláh's more intricate Arabic compositions – especially His poetry – are said to be virtually impossible to translate. It is no simple task to capture, in an alien tongue, the subtle rhythms and nuances that bring language vividly to life. Those of us who cannot read Arabic must therefore rely for insight upon those who can, just as students of the Bible, unless they understand Greek or Hebrew, must obtain much of their knowledge from scholars able to study the original manuscripts.

Literary Arabic traditionally incorporates subtle wordplay, often involving the deliberate breaking of grammatical rules to achieve a desired effect. The Qur'án, which Arabs regard as the ultimate stylistic model, employs this technique throughout with superb finesse. This is harder than it may sound: Anyone who attempts it without knowing precisely what he is doing will butcher the language, producing text that is clumsy or even incomprehensible. In some of His works, Bahá'u'lláh upholds textbook standards with scrupulous consistency, while in others He manipulates or disregards them at will – always enhancing the eloquence of His message by so doing.

Bahá'u'lláh's Persian writing was as exquisite and technically competent as His Arabic. This fact, however, is less surprising because Persian was His native language and one in which (unlike Arabic) He received some childhood tutoring. His choice of Arabic for many of His most important works was appropriate on several counts. First, Arabic traditionally is regarded in Islamic countries (including Persia) as the "language of revelation" since it is used in the Qur'án. Second, the Qur'án itself – a book of almost magical beauty, and one that laid the foundation for a mighty civilization – is revered in Islam as a literary miracle because Muḥammad, its author, was illiterate. Bahá'u'lláh of course was not illiterate in Arabic; but by human standards He should have been. By matching Muḥammad's achievement, He produced the one sign that, above all others, had for centuries been hailed by His countrymen as the most incontrovertible proof of prophetic authenticity. Finally, Persia's Islamic clergy (most of whose members inevitably opposed Him) had taken Arabic as their own primary badge of learning, a badge they struggled endlessly to polish. When Bahá'u'lláh, meeting them in their own chosen arena, effortlessly dwarfed their highest attainments, He not only caused consternation within their ranks but exposed the hollowness of their opposition.

A Torrent of Eloquence

A third token of the superhuman origin and nature of Bahá'u'lláh's knowledge is the seemingly impossible speed and spontaneity with which He composed His writings. Further enumerating the "signs" of His father's prophetic authenticity, 'Abdu'l-Bahá writes:

THE OBJECT OF ALL KNOWLEDGE

"Another of His signs is the marvel of His discourse, the eloquence of His utterance, the rapidity with which His Writings were revealed. . . . By thy very life! This thing is plain as day to whoever will regard it with the eye of justice." (SWA 15)

This phenomenon – documented both by eyewitness accounts and by empirical evidence – is one that no amount of education could adequately explain.

Any human mind, however great its capacity, is finite and fallible unless aided by some higher power. It follows that writing is a trial-and-error procedure for any normal author. Some writers, to be sure, are extremely prolific; a few of these are able to work long hours at high speed and produce relatively good work much of the time. But even for this select minority, serious writing involves certain necessities. These include preliminary thought and research, occasional hesitation and backtracking, and a certain amount of polishing and revision. Any composition a writer dashes off without these essential steps will be, at best, a "rough draft." Such work – however fine it may be overall – will show wide variations in quality, more or less obvious lapses in consistency and organization, and a general lack of attention to detail. The entire history of secular literature demonstrates that no ordinary human author, composing extemporaneously, can create perfectly finished work at all times and under all conditions.

So much for human writing. But what of revelation – a form of composition which, if it exists at all, must by definition emanate from an infinite, all-powerful, all-knowing, and perfect Intelligence? Presumably such a Being, transcending time and space and combining all-encompassing knowledge with boundless creativity, could know in advance precisely what He wished to convey through His human intermediary and how to formulate that message most befittingly to produce any desired effect.

The manner in which Bahá'u'lláh's writings were composed is therefore highly significant. Most of His "writings" are not, strictly speaking, writings at all: They were dictated by Him to one or more secretaries, who would later recopy them. Bahá'u'lláh would then verify the accuracy of the transcripts and affix His seal or signature. During dictation the words would cascade from His lips in a steady stream so rapidly as to tax the abilities of the most gifted stenographer. He seldom had any opportunity for prior reflection or rehearsal, since the bulk of His work consists of replies to letters He had not seen or heard until moments before He began to speak. During dictation He did not grope for words, lose His train of thought, or, having spoken, retract one phrase in order to substitute another.

After the secretary's notes were neatly recopied, Bahá'u'lláh, in checking the final version, would sometimes add margin notes or correct a word or two that had been transcribed incorrectly. In so doing, however, He did not revise or polish His own actual utterances.* When the workload was heavy and time short, He would sometimes dispense with the step of checking the transcript Himself. Instead, He would dictate the Tablet a second time from memory while the secretary followed along, proofreading the transcript from Bahá'u'lláh's utterances. (Adib Taherzadeh, "The Station of Bahá'u'lláh", a tape-recorded talk delivered in 1987 in Brazil)

Until the end of His life, Bahá'u'lláh poured out His writings in sessions that often lasted for hours at a time. Within two days and nights, for example, He composed the Kitáb-i-Íqán, or Book of Certitude, one of His major works: Its English translation exceeds 250 pages. Most of these writings He produced under conditions of bitter adversity, often when He was weak from hunger, illness, or exhaustion, stricken with grief, harassed by enemies, or mortally endangered by their schemes. He Himself describes His words as "a copious rain" (GPB 133), commenting: "Such are the outpourings . . . from the clouds of Divine Bounty that within the space of an hour the equivalent of a thousand verses hath been revealed." (ibid. 171)

A believer named Siyyid Asadu'lláh-i-Qumí, who was present during some of these sessions, left the following account:

"I recall that as Mírzá Áqá Ján [Bahá'u'lláh's primary secretary] was recording the words of Bahá'u'lláh at the time of revelation, the shrill sound of his pen could be heard from a distance of about twenty paces. . . .

"Mírzá Áqá Ján had a large ink-pot the size of a small bowl. He also had available about ten to twelve pens and large sheets of paper in

---

*Bahá'u'lláh sometimes would adapt His own previous works to a new context by means of minor editing. In publishing, for example, a general-audience version of a Tablet revealed earlier for an individual, He might change tense or gender, omit personal references, clarify allusions that would have been obvious to His original recipient, and so forth. Thus we sometimes have two authentic yet subtly different versions of the same Tablet (the Book of Certitude being a case in point). Their triviality aside, however, such variations serve generally obvious purposes having nothing to do with the merit of the work in question. In this respect they differ fundamentally from the corrective rewriting in which most authors (including, of course, myself) compulsively engage.

stacks. In those days all letters which arrived for Bahá'u'lláh were received by Mírzá Áqá Ján. He would bring these into the presence of Bahá'u'lláh and, having obtained permission, would read them. Afterwards [Bahá'u'lláh] would direct him to take up his pen and record the Tablet which was revealed in reply. . . .

"Such was the speed with which he used to write the revealed Word that the ink of the first word was scarcely yet dry when the whole page was finished. It seemed as if someone had dipped a lock of hair in the ink and applied it over the whole page. None of the words was written clearly and they were illegible to all except Mírzá Áqá Ján. There were occasions when even he could not decipher the words and had to seek the help of Bahá'u'lláh. When revelation had ceased, then . . . Mírzá Áqá Ján would rewrite the Tablet in his best hand and dispatch it to its destination. . . ." (quoted in Taherzadeh, *Revelation,* vol. I, pp. 35-6)

Nabíl-i-A'ẓam, a Bahá'í historian who accompanied Bahá'u'lláh throughout much of His exile and imprisonment, and who chronicled both his own firsthand observations and the eyewitness accounts of others, shares the following details:

"A number of secretaries were busy day and night and yet they were unable to cope with the task. Among them was Mírzá Báqir-i-Shírází. . . . He alone transcribed no less than two thousand verses every day. He labored during six or seven months. Every month the equivalent of several volumes would be transcribed by him and sent to Persia. About twenty volumes, in his fine penmanship, he left behind as a remembrance. . . ." (quoted in GPB 171)

Many other observers have left similar accounts. However, we need not rely entirely on their testimony to verify this phenomenon. After Bahá'u'lláh's Tablets were dispatched, the original notes of Mírzá Áqá Ján and other secretaries were generally distributed to resident Bahá'ís and visiting pilgrims as souvenirs. The early believers treasured these keepsakes and called them "revelation writing." Countless specimens of this stenography have since been collected at the Bahá'í World Center. To appreciate the value of these historical documents, simply suppose the disciples of Christ had taken notes as He spoke and had preserved them for study by future generations of scholars. Handwritten dictation, scribbled frantically without pause by a secretary working under high pressure, looks much the same in any language. The "revelation writing" therefore bears eloquent testimony to the circumstances of its origin. By comparing its almost illegible scrawl with careful Arabic or Persian penmanship, anyone – even knowing nothing of the languages – can visualize the speed and continuity with which Bahá'u'-lláh's secretaries worked. (For photostatic copies of "revelation writing," see page 110 of Adib Taherzadeh's *The Revelation of Bahá'u'lláh*, vol. I. Contrast them with any sample of legible Arabic penmanship, such as the neatly transcribed Tablet reproduced as the frontispiece of the same book.)

The torrential flow of Bahá'u'lláh's utterance could more easily be explained away if the resulting writings were occasionally of lackluster quality. Such is not the case, however. The caliber of His work is not only strikingly uniform but uniformly superlative. This of course does not mean His writings are all alike; one of the very things that makes them excellent is the astounding diversity they incorporate. "At one time," says Bahá'u'lláh, "We spoke in the language of the lawgiver; at another in that of the truth seeker and the mystic. . . ." (ibid. 217) However, all His compositions are from beginning to end highly polished, meticulously organized, lucidly presented, and vibrant with spiritual power and beauty.

There are various standards by which to judge quality in writing; some of these – such as eloquence or beauty – will vary considerably according to individual taste. Other yardsticks are not so flexible. If, for instance, an author quotes from the works of others, or even from his own works, we are entitled to ask how accurately he has done so. Bahá'u'lláh would some-times quote liberally from scriptures of past religions, or from works by sages, mystics, historians, and the like. Many of these excerpts are from obscure or little-known works to which He seemingly had no access at the time; He could not, in any event, have stopped to look them up without interrupting His pacing and His dictation. Both the original notes and eyewitness reports indicate that He always dictated these passages afresh: He did not simply instruct the secretary to look up the necessary text and insert it. Sometimes verification of His sources required hours or even months of research by scholars. Bahá'u'lláh's citations are always scrupulously precise. So rigorous is His use of such secondary material that we would never know (if the historical record were less clear) that we are reading extemporaneous composition.

Closing Comments

This chapter explored further the issue of whether Bahá'u'lláh displayed knowledge not readily available to Him through normal human channels. It attempted to do so in ways that look beyond the various historical and scientific prophecies detailed in previous chapters. To restate the main points:

Bahá'u'lláh spent His crucial formative years in an atmosphere of profound superstition and prejudice, receiving only the most perfunctory education. Despite these disadvantages, His knowledge aroused the wonder and admiration of many eminent scholars. Three especially striking features of that knowledge testify to its intuitive and seemingly superhuman character: (1) His farsightedness – Bahá'u'lláh in His writings analyzed and foreshadowed all the sweeping social changes of the twentieth century, displaying a thorough grasp of future global policy issues that had not yet even begun to engage the attention of His contemporaries. (2) His mastery of Arabic literary writing – He demonstrated, apparently without study or training, a flawless command of this highly technical subject, which normally takes many years of drill and discipline to acquire. (3) His creative speed and spontaneity – He consistently produced highly polished, superbly organized, deeply thoughtful writing embellished with exact quotes from a wide variety of sources at phenomenal speed in completely extemporaneous fashion.

This chapter has said nothing, until now, about the Báb or 'Abdu'l-Bahá. Because Bahá'u'lláh Himself teaches that both these men also were divinely illumined (the Báb directly, as a Manifestation of God, and 'Abdu'l-Bahá indirectly, as the Perfect Exemplar and appointed Interpreter of the Faith), it is fair to ask whether They showed similar signs of innate knowledge.

Any thoughtful student of Bahá'í history will discover such signs in abundance. Since a detailed discussion of these issues would extend far beyond the useful length of this book, the reader is referred to the bibliography for more information. Briefly, however, I will say that while the outward circumstances differ, they paint the same picture in each case: All three Central Figures of the Bahá'í Faith manifested an apparently intuitive grasp of skills and subjects entirely foreign to Their backgrounds, and all three displayed the same torrential spontaneity in composing perfectly polished text. ('Abdu'l-Bahá, when pressed for time, would dictate to as many as five secretaries at once, moving rapidly from one to another, speaking of different subjects and even using different languages, without ever losing the thread of His thought.)

Do these observations prove Bahá'u'lláh was a Messenger from God? Certainly not – not in any everyday sense of the word "prove." In religion, as in science, there is never any fact or body of facts, however large, that cannot be explained in more than one way. So long as we can explain our findings in more than one way, we can never "prove" absolutely which explanation is correct. All we can do is try to weigh the evidence as fairly as possible and exercise our best judgment. I have tried in this chapter to sharpen the focus, to present facts which, added to the successful historical and scientific predictions described in previous chapters, simplify such a decision.

However, the facts are not all in. All information we have discussed so far has pertained, directly or otherwise, to the question of Bahá'u'lláh's knowledge. Important as this may be, knowledge is not the only, or even the most important, characteristic we should expect to find in a Divine Manifestation. The next chapter will discuss some of these other characteristics and will suggest ways to test for them that could shed light on our central question: *Who was Bahá'u'lláh?*

Chapter Six

THE SUN: ITS OWN PROOF

He Who is everlastingly hidden from the eyes of men can never be known except through His Manifestation, and His Manifestation can adduce no greater proof of the truth of His Mission than the proof of His own Person.

—*Bahá'u'lláh*

. . . the Sun of Righteousness [shall] arise, with healing in His wings.

—*Malachi 4:2*

WE HAVE BEEN EXPLORING the claim of Bahá'u'lláh by repeatedly asking two questions. First, what phenomena may reasonably be expected to occur if His claim is true? Second, do those phenomena actually occur?

To sum up the main points so far: Anyone claiming to be a Manifestation of God (as the term is defined by Bahá'u'lláh) must be, among other things, "omniscient at will." Such a person should be able correctly to describe events of the future. Bahá'u'lláh did this. Such a person should understand scientific facts not yet discovered in His time. Bahá'u'lláh did this. Such a person should possess skills not acquired in, or even available from, any school and display a deep understanding of spiritual and social problems beyond the experience of His learned contemporaries. Bahá'u'lláh did these things.

But a Manifestation of God, if such a Being exists at all, cannot be merely a fountain of knowledge. An individual might conceivably be a walking encyclopedia, able to divulge all manner of fascinating and useful information, and still lack many other admirable qualities such as compassion, fairness, humor, courage, or many others. No such person could be considered a Manifestation of God in the Bahá'í sense. The periodic Manifestations, according to Bahá'u'lláh, fully reflect the infinite perfections of the Creator Himself: They are "endowed with all the attributes of God, such as sovereignty, dominion, and the like. . . ." (G 49) Whatever They do or say is what God would do or say were He to appear in human form. Beyond this, They are Spiritual Suns, ablaze with divine energy powerful enough to transform the world and redirect its history for hundreds or even thousands of years. They "manifest" God as a flawless mirror manifests or reflects the sun. Christ Himself – the "Word made Flesh" – said no less: "If ye had known Me, ye should have known My Father also." (John 14:7)

It follows that any true Manifestation of God must be extraordinary in ways that go far beyond intellectual attainment. As the exponent and representative of God on earth, He is not literally God, but His presence is in a very real sense the presence of God. What would such a presence be like? How would it feel to enter the company of a Divine Manifestation, to converse and interact with Him and thus obtain a glimpse of His true nature?

Perhaps the first thing we must say about such questions is that we can never truly know the answers – not, at least, without first having had the experience. Since we ordinarily have no direct contact with infinite perfection, we cannot logically hope to imagine such contact in any realistic way. This very futility, however, allows us to say one thing with considerable assurance: To be in the presence of a Manifestation must be a rare experience indeed, unforgettable and indescribable. Presumably it would be unlike any other experience on earth. We may reasonably expect that the personality of a Manifestation of God should make an overpowering impression and should have a lasting impact on persons who encounter Him – even on those of high rank and capacity.

Since Bahá'u'lláh left this earth in 1892, we can no longer physically enter His presence and thus judge firsthand how well He satisfied these expectations. The best we can do is study the reactions of those who met Him and try to see Him through their eyes. This does not mean we should substitute their judgment for our own, nor does it bind us to accept their explanations of what they experienced. (Different witnesses, in any case, explained their experiences in different and sometimes contradictory ways.) Just the same, such a study is clearly relevant for anyone wishing to evaluate Bahá'u'lláh's claim in systematic fashion. We can say, at the very least, that if someone claims to be a Manifestation of God, but ordinarily makes no unusual impression on those who meet him and demonstrates no extraordinary qualities of character, that person's claim must be considered suspect. If the opposite is true, then, by the same token, that impression and those qualities must to some extent strengthen his claim.

THE PROOF OF HIS PERSON

As previous chapters have indicated, the life of Bahá'u'lláh is extensively documented. His photograph, surrounded by a wide array of personal effects, is reverently displayed in the Archives Building at the Bahá'í World Center in Haifa. Thousands of people met Him – believers and skeptics, rich and poor, high government officials, noted scholars, and ordinary people from all walks of life. These individuals left unnumbered public records, diplomatic papers, diaries, memoirs, interviews, oral histories, and anecdotes reflecting His movements and activities on an almost daily basis. What can we learn from such documentation?

His Magnetic Presence

From this array of primary source material, one fact leaps out again and again, at every turn and in every possible way. That fact is Bahá'u'lláh's spellbinding personal magnetism. "An atmosphere of majesty," says 'Abdu'l-Bahá, "haloed Him as the sun at midday." (GPB 124) The almost irresistible charm of His personality thrilled His friends and confused His enemies; the latter warned inquirers to avoid Him lest they become mesmerized by His "sorcery." Complete strangers, knowing nothing of His station or identity, would often bow spontaneously on the occasion of a surprise meeting. High-ranking skeptics and cynics, accustomed to dealing on an equal footing with notables of every description, would become awestruck and speechless in His presence. His loyal followers, having known Him, could not bear to be separated from Him; many abandoned lives of comfort and affluence in order to share His exile and imprisonment. His hard-boiled jailers and custodians routinely became devoted admirers, placing their resources at His disposal and offering to help Him escape – offers He would kindly but firmly refuse.

"If you had come to this blessed place ['Akká] in the days of the manifestation of the evident Light," says 'Abdu'l-Bahá,

> *"if you had attained to the court of His presence, and had witnessed His luminous beauty, you would have understood that His teachings and perfection were not in need of further evidence.*
>
> *"Only through the honor of entering His presence, many souls became confirmed believers; they had no need of other proofs. Even those people who rejected and hated Him bitterly, when they had met Him, would testify to the grandeur of Bahá'u'lláh, saying: 'This is a magnificent man, but what a pity that He makes such a claim! Otherwise, all that He says is acceptable.'"* (SAQ 36)

Hájí Mírzá Haydar-'Alí, a Bahá'í residing in 'Akká who witnessed many such encounters, comments as follows:

> *"Although [Bahá'u'lláh] showed much compassion and loving-kindness, and approached anyone who came to His presence with tender care and humbleness, and often used to make humorous remarks to put them at ease, yet in spite of these, no one, whether faithful or disbelieving,*

learned or unlettered, wise or foolish, was able to utter ten words in His presence in the usual everyday manner. Indeed, many would find themselves to be tremulous with an impediment in their speech.

"Some people asked permission to attain His presence for the sole purpose of conducting arguments and engaging in controversies. As a favor on His part, and in order to fulfill the testimony and to declare conclusively the proofs, He gave these permission to enter the court of His majesty and glory. As they entered the room, heard His voice welcoming them in, and gazed at His countenance beaming with the light of grandeur, they could not help but prostrate themselves at His door. They would then enter and sit down. When He showed them where to sit, they would find themselves unable to utter a word or put forward their questions. When they left they would bow to Him involuntarily. Some would be transformed through the influence of meeting Him and would leave with the utmost sincerity and devotion, some would depart as admirers, while others would leave His presence, ignorant and heedless, attributing their experience to pure sorcery. . . . To be brief, the bounties which were vouchsafed to a person as a result of attaining His presence were indescribable and unknowable. The proof of the sun is the sun itself." (quoted in Taherzadeh, *Revelation,* vol. III, pp. 247-9)

One of the most overworked and debased words in the English language is "charisma" – a word currently applied to any performer with crowd appeal and to every politician or preacher with an engaging personality. To any thoughtful student of Bahá'u'lláh's life, it will be obvious that His uncanny effect on others was of an entirely different and higher order. Much of what passes today for charisma is actually the work of "image consultants" who teach their clients how to manipulate news media, stage publicity stunts, "dress for success," and surround themselves with symbols of leadership and authority. Bahá'u'lláh did none of these things. He lived frugally, wore simple clothing, conducted Himself in a modest and unassuming manner, and (despite His audacious claim) avoided the limelight. Such was His radiance of spirit, however, that those who felt its warmth often remarked they felt transported to paradise.

Few if any firsthand descriptions of Bahá'u'lláh dwell on details of His physical appearance. Instead, they speak of such things as His kingly dignity, His flashing eyes and penetrating gaze, and His melodious voice that always carried a sense of calm authority. Time and again such reports mention the ineffable sense of serenity and exhilaration one felt in His presence. Perhaps the best-known pen portrait of Bahá'u'lláh is the following account by

Edward Granville Browne, the distinguished Cambridge Orientalist who met Him at 'Akká in 1890:

"Though I dimly suspected whither I was going and whom I was to behold (for no distinct intimation had been given to me), a second or two elapsed ere, with a throb of wonder and awe, I became definitely conscious that the room was not untenanted. In the corner where the divan met the wall sat a wondrous and venerable figure, crowned with a felt head-dress of the kind called taj *by dervishes (but of unusual height and make), round the base of which was wound a small white turban. The face of him on whom I gazed I can never forget, though I cannot describe it. Those piercing eyes seemed to read one's very soul; power and authority sat on that ample brow; while the deep lines on the forehead and face implied an age which the jet-black hair and beard flowing down in indistinguishable luxuriance almost to the waist seemed to belie. No need to ask in whose presence I stood, as I bowed myself before one who is the object of a devotion and love which kings might envy and emperors sigh for in vain!"* (quoted in Taherzadeh, *Revelation,* vol. II, pp. 12-13)

Many specific incidents could be culled from Bahá'u'lláh's life story to illustrate His awe-inspiring majesty and the various reactions it evoked. One extreme instance occurred when the Persian consul-general in Baghdad hired a Turkish ruffian named Riḍá to assassinate Bahá'u'lláh. Armed with a pistol, Riḍá tried twice to carry out his mission – once by approaching the Bahá'í leader in a public bath and again by lying in ambush for Him as He walked the city's streets. Both times, when actually confronting his prey, the assassin lost his nerve. On the second occasion he became so frightened and bewildered that he dropped his weapon; whereupon an amused Bahá'u'lláh instructed that the pistol be handed back to him and arranged for an escort to help the dazed man find his way home! (Shoghi Effendi, GPB 142) (Riḍá himself, in later years, circulated this story.)

The electrifying impact of Bahá'u'lláh's presence is clear not only from the testimony of His followers, but also – in an ironic and backhanded way – from that of Muslim and Christian clergymen seeking to discredit Him. Realizing that this phenomenon required an explanation, His detractors labored to supply one that would not enhance the credibility of His prophetic claim. One oft-repeated theory was that visitors were carefully conditioned in advance to see Bahá'u'lláh as a godlike being. Each pilgrim was told (so the story went) that what he would experience depended on his own spiritual capacity: A material being would see Bahá'u'lláh only as a man, but a sufficiently spiritual one would see God. Only after the visitor had been aroused to a frenzy of anticipation (the story continued) would he be allowed, for a few moments, to enter the Holy Presence and gaze adoringly at the face of his Lord. The almost magical effect of such visits was thus attributed to psychological manipulation.

This superficially plausible explanation might well convince someone who had only minimal knowledge about Bahá'u'lláh; it cannot, however, stand up to serious examination. Its fictitious character is clearly exposed by the testimony of many credible and independent eyewitnesses. E. G. Browne, for example, whose soul-stirring encounter with Bahá'u'lláh is quoted above, was aware of this cynical theory but recognized it as nonsense. He himself, as noted above, says he only "dimly suspected" he was being taken to see Bahá'u'lláh, "for no distinct intimation had been given" to him. Browne, though not a believer in Bahá'u'lláh's claim, was a friend, but reactions similar to his were commonplace even among those who initially were far less receptive. As Hájí Mírzá Haydar-'Alí comments:

> *"When a believer describes what he has experienced in the presence of Bahá'u'lláh, his impressions may be interpreted as being formed through his attitude of self-effacement and a feeling of utter nothingness in relation to Him. But to what can it be attributed when one enters into His presence as an antagonist and leaves as a believer, or comes in as an enemy but goes out as a friend, or comes to raise controversial arguments, but departs without saying anything and, due to willful blindness, attributing this to magic?"* (quoted in Taherzadeh, *Revelation*, vol. III, p. 249

Bahá'u'lláh's Muslim opponents were painfully aware of His power to bewitch even those who were hostile or indifferent. Aside from warning inquirers to avoid His presence and avoiding it themselves, they introduced a further explanation for these reactions by nonbelievers. Their idea was, quite simply, that Bahá'u'lláh and His followers administered hypnotic drugs to their contacts. Elaborate refinements were added as the story spread: The drug – purportedly an "extract of dates" – was said to be slipped into the delicious Persian tea customarily served to guests at Bahá'u'lláh's home. For those too wise to accept the spiked tea, there supposedly was a further stratagem: The drug would be compressed into a tiny pill and, at an opportune moment, surreptitiously tossed into the visitor's open mouth. The hypno-drug theory, ludicrous though it was, was widely aired and believed in Persia for a number of decades.

This chapter has so far discussed only Bahá'u'lláh, arguing that His stupendous personal magnetism was consistent with His claim fully to reveal and manifest the infinite perfections of God. He demonstrated precisely those signs we should expect to see in Him if that claim is true. This raises a further question: What of the Báb, Whose own claim to be a Manifestation is endorsed by Bahá'u'lláh Himself? If Bahá'u'lláh was genuine, then the Báb was genuine, and we should expect to observe in Him the same remarkable signs.

On this question the facts of history are, once again, too clear to invite serious debate. The Báb's presence, like that of Bahá'u'lláh, was by all accounts riveting; it affected even indifferent or apathetic onlookers like a thunderbolt. Having experienced it, many former opponents preferred to die rather than part from Him or deny their belief. His enemies, like bats fleeing from light, steered clear of Him and warned others to do the same lest they fall under His spell.

Reverend T. K. Cheyne, a well-known Oxford Bible scholar, wrote of the Báb:

"His combination of mildness and power is so rare that we have to place him in a line with super-normal men. . . . We learn that, at great points in His career, after he had been in an ecstasy, such radiance of might and majesty streamed from his countenance that none could bear to look upon the effulgence of his glory and beauty. Nor was it an uncommon occurrence for unbelievers involuntarily to bow down in lowly obeisance on beholding His Holiness. . . . " (Cheyne, *The Reconciliation of Races and Religions,* pp. 7-9, quoted by Shoghi Effendi in DB p. 516n)

Joseph Arthur le Comte de Gobineau, one of the first European historians to investigate the story of the Báb in depth, writes that He was "of extreme simplicity of manner, of a fascinating gentleness, those gifts were further heightened by his great youth and his marvelous charm. . . . He could not open his lips (we are assured by those who knew him) without stirring the hearts to their very depths." (Gobineau, *Religions* 118, quoted by Shoghi Effendi in DB 79-80n4) Furthermore, Gobineau writes, "Those who came near him felt in spite of themselves the fascinating influence of his personality, of his manner and of his speech. His guards were not free from that weakness." (ibid. 502n) Concerning the Báb's effect on unbelievers, Gobineau says: ". . . even the orthodox Muhammadans who were present [at encounters with Him] have retained an indelible memory of them and never recall them without a sort of terror. They agreed unanimously that [His] eloquence . . . was of an incomparable kind, such that, without having been an eyewitness, one could not possibly imagine." (ibid. 157n)

Of the Bahá'í Faith's three Central Figures, 'Abdu'l-Bahá is in many ways the most paradoxical. He is not regarded by Bahá'ís as a Manifestation of God, and He never for a moment pretended to be cut from the same cloth as the Báb and Bahá'u'lláh. Still, if Bahá'u'lláh was a reflection of God, 'Abdu'l-Bahá was in some sense a reflection and extension of Bahá'u'lláh, Who called Him "the Gulf that hath branched out of this Ocean that hath encompassed all created things" (GPB 243). From texts already cited, it should be clear that just as Bahá'u'lláh's spiritual majesty towered above that of His son, so must that of His son (if the Faith's claims be true) have towered above that of humanity in general.

'Abdu'l-Bahá was, to Western eyes, the most accessible of the Faith's major figures. His travels throughout America, as well as His visits to Canada, the United Kingdom, France, Germany, Austria, and Hungary, brought Him into direct contact with the Western press and public, as well as with numerous dignitaries and leaders of thought. It is fair to say that wherever He went, He was mobbed by enthusiastic admirers, most of whom had never before heard of Him. Judging from the crowds that thronged His public talks and from the sensational press coverage that followed His every move, one would have thought He was a world-class celebrity – not the obscure head of an even more obscure Eastern religion. The volumes of prose written by those who remembered Him reflect a clear consensus as to His remarkable qualities. One could hardly summarize that consensus more aptly than by quoting these words of Mrs. Phoebe Hearst (mother of William Randolph Hearst): "Tho He does not seek to impress one at all, strength, power, purity, love and holiness are radiated from His majestic, yet humble, personality, and the spiritual atmosphere which surrounds Him and most powerfully affects all those who are blest by being near Him, is indescribable." (quoted in Balyuzi, *'Abdu'l-Bahá* 70-1) Another recurring comment was that merely to sit beside Him in an automobile, even when He was physically exhausted from His hectic speaking schedule, was to feel oneself being charged with spiritual energy.

'Abdu'l-Bahá always insisted that He was but a drop compared to Bahá'u'lláh's ocean. However, those who knew only the son often found it difficult to conceive that His father (or anyone else) could have surpassed His transcendent majesty or His irresistible power of attraction. In one of His Tablets, 'Abdu'l-Bahá asks us to contemplate, in light of His own astounding impact on Westerners, what might have been achieved by the One who was immeasurably greater:

"How foolish are the people of the East to have incarcerated for well-nigh fifty years the like of this glorious personage! But for His chains and prison, Bahá'u'lláh by this time would have gained absolute ascendancy over the minds and thoughts of the peoples of Europe. . . . Consider and reflect upon the result of My few days in London and the profound effect it has had here and in the surrounding regions. Ponder then in your heart, what the coming of Bahá'u'lláh would have achieved! Had He appeared in Europe, its people would have seized their opportunity, and His Cause, by virtue of the freedom of thought, would by this time have encompassed the earth. But, alas! This Cause, though it first appeared in Persia, yet eventually it shall be seen how the peoples of Europe have wrested it from its hands! Take note of this and remember it in future. Ultimately you shall see how it has come to pass. And yet behold! how the Bahá'ís are still persecuted by the people of Persia!"
(translated by Shoghi Effendi and transmitted 12 January 1923 to the National Spiritual Assembly of the Bahá'ís of the United States; quoted in Marcella, *Quest for Eden* 261-2)

As stated above, we can no longer physically meet such remarkable beings as Bahá'u'lláh, the Báb and 'Abdu'l-Bahá; thus we cannot experience for ourselves the dynamic influence Their presence is said to have exerted. We are free to explain in any way we like the subjective reactions of others. But we cannot deny, as a matter of historical fact, what those reactions were; nor can we doubt that such reactions were typical not only of believers but of unbelievers – people of capacity whose impressions can in no way be ascribed to simpleminded credulity. We may well ask ourselves: What manner of being can consistently produce so unforgettable an impact upon human consciousness, and how can we explain the successive appearance of three such extraordinary beings, closely linked as Central Figures of one world faith?

Certainly the answers to these questions are not so self-evident as to force acceptance of Bahá'u'lláh's claim. Still, the observations that prompt such questions clearly have some bearing upon, and relevance to, the probable truth or falsity of that claim. The nature of that bearing and relevance is of course for each inquirer to judge, impartially and independently.

His Luminous Character
Another way to test the claim of any purported Divine Messenger is to examine the claimant's character. What can we learn about the moral and ethical stature of the candidate? Like the other issues we have been considering, unusual nobility of character falls short of "proving" in any absolute

sense that its possessor is a Manifestation of God. Lack of such nobility, however, would most assuredly prove someone was not. Therein lies the question's importance. The Manifestations must be more than "good people": They are, by definition, beings who fully personify all the divine attributes. Since one of those attributes, presumably, is moral perfection, it stands to reason that any genuine Manifestation must exemplify an exalted standard of conduct that few people would be able to uphold.

We must exercise care in approaching this issue. One thorny obstacle is deciding how to define character. Throughout history, followers of every faith have applied their own standards to the founders of other faiths and judged those founders defective. Jews criticized Jesus for breaking the Sabbath. Christians condemned Muḥammad for taking several wives and for defending His religion by force of arms. Muslims expressed moral outrage when Bahá'u'lláh established equality of women with men. Examples could be multiplied without end.

Bahá'ís reply that it is not man but God Who, through His Manifestation, reveals the social norms and moral values that are to prevail until the coming of a new Manifestation. Right and wrong are whatever He says they are, until His Dispensation ends: The Manifestation "doeth whatsoever He willeth, and ordaineth whatsoever He pleaseth" (KI 97); moreover, "He shall not be asked of His doings." (ibid. 171) Being guided by God, each Manifestation is free to keep the law of His predecessor, modify it, or discard it altogether as He deems appropriate. This in no way implies that divine revelation is arbitrary: 'Abdu'l-Bahá says, "The Laws of God are not imposition of will, or of power, or pleasure, but the resolutions of truth, reason and justice." (PT 154) The point is that God sees the entire puzzle while we see only pieces; therefore only He can correctly weigh the infinite variables and decide, based on the circumstances of history and man's spiritual readiness, what will best promote human development in a given period.

It may seem, at first glance, that this concept denies by implication the very possibility of evaluating the character of anyone claiming to be a Divine Manifestation. If He and He alone defines the standard by which He is to be judged, all previous criteria being ruled out of order, will He not appear to be a saint whether His claim is true or false? The answer is, "Not necessarily." In theory, this may seem to be a problem; but in practice it resolves itself quite neatly for two reasons.

First, the teachings of religion fall into two quite different categories: social laws and spiritual principles. Social laws cover marriage and divorce, dietary practices, devotional observances, the lending of money, treatment of criminals, governmental policies, and thousands of other practical concerns. These laws are subject to change in every revelation. For instance, the dietary restrictions and penal code of Moses, perfectly tailored to the nomadic heritage of the Children of Israel, were no longer appropriate by the time of Jesus; Christianity therefore modified them. Fundamental spiritual principles, however, are quite another matter. While different faiths employ different terminologies to express them, these principles are the same in every religious dispensation: They rest on truths that are eternal and immutable. The Golden Rule, for example, is central to the holy scriptures of every religion. The same may be said of exhortations to love, kindness, justice, mercy, patience, courtesy, cleanliness, honesty, self-discipline, and the like. Attributes such as these clearly derive their importance from the inward, eternal aspect of religious morality and not from the outward, temporary social aspect. These unnumbered virtues are of course the same in the teachings of Bahá'u'lláh as in the teachings of Abraham, Christ, or Buddha.

Second, Bahá'u'lláh Himself stipulates that a Manifestation of God is the first to put His own teachings into practice: ". . . whatsoever thou dost behold in His deeds, the same wilt thou find in His sayings, and whatsoever thou dost read in His sayings, that wilt thou recognize in His deeds." (KI 57) For a Manifestation of God or anyone else to behave in this way is no small accomplishment, particularly when the standard He inculcates is uncommonly lofty and challenging. History is filled with examples of wise men and philosophers who preached one thing while practicing another. No one whose deeds and words are in manifest conflict can plausibly claim to be a Manifestation of God, as Bahá'ís understand the term.

These considerations suggest two ways in which we can study the personal characters of Bahá'u'lláh, the Báb, and 'Abdu'l-Bahá. First, disregarding for the moment whether we agree with Their social principles, we can ask how fully They exemplified those eternal qualities of spirit upheld as essential in all religions. Second, we can ask how consistent Their behavior was with Their own teachings, remembering that only the rarest individuals act as nobly as they speak. These two questions, of course, overlap considerably; for many purposes they are simply different ways of looking at a single yardstick.

Studying Bahá'u'lláh's life from this perspective, we see clearly that the deep devotion He inspired was due to more than the force of His personality or the sublimity of His teachings. It followed, just as surely, from His exemplary personal life and rectitude of conduct. The common thread tying together all the diverse events of His life was this: He was forced to choose, on an almost daily basis, between His own welfare and that of others. In literally every instance, He sacrificed Himself for the betterment of humanity.

Scores of incidents and anecdotes illustrate this theme; we have space here to touch only the barest highlights. It is well known that sometime before the declaration of the Báb, Bahá'u'lláh had turned down the lucrative government post previously occupied by His late father, Mírzá Buzurg. Instead, He devoted His considerable fortune entirely to charitable and humanitarian work. He and His wife Navváb, who shared His priorities, were known to the masses as the "Father of the Poor" and the "Mother of Consolation." Public officials and the clergy (not yet faced with the challenge of accepting or rejecting Him as the Promised One) also held him in high esteem but warned Him that His continued generosity towards the poor would soon impoverish Him.

The point became moot when Bahá'u'lláh espoused the cause of the Báb, for so bold and public a stance seemed tantamount to suicide. His reputation, however, protected Him until state-sponsored persecution boiled over in the massacres that followed the Báb's martyrdom. Even then, He could have chosen safety, for the anti-Bábí hysteria erupted during a time when He was away from home, visiting the brother of the prime minister. Friends in the country offered to hide Him until the storm abated. Spurning their offer, Bahá'u'lláh headed for the capital to confront the foes of the Faith, turning Himself in along the way to a military detail sent to arrest Him. He was conducted "on foot and in chains, with bared head and bare feet" (ESW 20) under the pitiless August sun, from the hill villages north of Tehran to the city's great dungeon. Along the way He was pelted with stones and filth by the crowds. At one point an old woman, wishing to play her part in punishing the vile heretic (as authorities now were depicting Him), ran alongside, begging the soldiers to pause long enough for her to cast her stone. Bahá'u'-lláh gave a revealing glimpse of His nature by telling the soldiers, "Suffer not this woman to be disappointed. Deny her not what she regards as a meritorious act in the sight of God." (DB 607-8) To cheer her blind and hardened heart, He then submitted patiently to the added injury.

While Bahá'u'lláh was personally forgiving, His forbearance and compassion sprang not from weakness but from deep strength. We are reminded of the way in which "gentle Jesus, meek and mild" used a bullwhip to clear the temple of moneychangers who had made of His Father's house a den of thieves. Bahá'u'lláh was lionlike in His defense of the Faith, routing His enemies in debate and brilliantly exposing their hypocrisy. Although He endured persecution when He had to do so to prosecute His mission, He never sought it out: Throughout His life, in fact, He strenuously protested the campaign of terror the authorities waged against Him and His followers. (In one instance, an outraged Bahá'u'lláh risked torture and death by rebuking the sultan of Turkey for the latter's cruelty to Bahá'í women and children.)

When Bahá'u'lláh entered the dungeon of Tehran – the unutterably foul "Black Pit" – He was in His mid-thirties and in the prime of health. He left it four months later an emaciated shadow, scarred for life. He had been forced, along with a number of other Bábís, to wear chains so heavy that they cut through to His collarbone; to eat food poisoned, at one point, by His enemies; to breathe air polluted with the stench of human waste and festering wounds; and to stay in a position that made sleep virtually impossible. Each day one of the Bábís would be taken out and executed, reminding the others that their turn might come next. Bahá'u'lláh and His fellow-prisoners fueled their courage by chanting songs of praise and glorification to God – songs that could be heard even in the palace of the sháh, some distance away.

In that dungeon in 1852, the conviction came to Bahá'u'lláh that He and He alone was the Promised One Whose imminent appearance the Báb had proclaimed. "One night in a dream," He wrote many years later,

"these exalted words were heard on every side: 'Verily, We shall render Thee victorious by Thyself and by Thy pen. Grieve Thou not for that which hath befallen Thee, neither be Thou afraid, for Thou art in safety. Ere long will God raise up the treasures of the earth – men who will aid Thee through Thyself and through Thy Name, wherewith God hath revived the hearts of such as have recognized Him.'" (GPB 101)

Bahá'u'lláh did not, until 1863, announce His claim to be the Redeemer foretold by the Báb. However, He referred to it often in barely veiled allusions contained in the odes, essays, and letters that began to flow from His pen immediately after His release from prison. At the same time, coinciding with His initial banishment to Baghdad, He arose to regenerate the devastated Bábí community. He succeeded, by precept and example, in transforming its members into the "treasures of the earth" who, as promised in His dream, would bring victory to the Cause of God.

Throughout the long years of exile, persecution, and imprisonment that followed, Bahá'u'lláh faced danger and hardship with superhuman fortitude. Wherever He went He earned a reputation as a great humanitarian, a man of deep compassion, truthfulness, and integrity. Even those who refused to accept His claims and doctrines frequently expressed admiration for His personal life; the words "saintly" and "Christ-like" appear frequently in their descriptions of Him. In the following admonition addressed to one of His sons, He clearly set forth the standard of which He was a walking embodiment:

"Be generous in prosperity, and thankful in adversity. Be worthy of the trust of thy neighbor, and look upon him with a bright and friendly face. Be a treasure to the poor, an admonisher to the rich, an answerer of the cry of the needy, a preserver of the sanctity of thy pledge. Be fair in thy judgment, and guarded in thy speech. Be unjust to no man, and show all meekness to all men. Be as a lamp unto them that walk in darkness, a joy to the sorrowful, a sea for the thirsty, a haven for the distressed, an upholder and defender of the victim of oppression. Let integrity and uprightness distinguish all thine acts. Be a home for the stranger, a balm to the suffering, a tower of strength for the fugitive. Be eyes to the blind, and a guiding light unto the feet of the erring. Be an ornament to the countenance of truth, a crown to the brow of fidelity, a pillar of the temple of righteousness, a breath of life to the body of mankind, an ensign of the hosts of justice, a luminary above the horizon of virtue, a dew to the soil of the human heart, an ark on the ocean of knowledge, a sun in the heaven of bounty, a gem on the diadem of wisdom, a shining light in the firmament of thy generation, a fruit upon the tree of humility."
(ESW, pp. 93-4)

The seamless consistency between Bahá'u'lláh's words and actions revealed itself in countless ways. He taught His followers, for example, to obey the laws and decrees of duly constituted governments (except in certain extremely grave matters of conscience; for example, a Bahá'í may not, even to save his own life, renounce his faith). Bahá'u'lláh Himself upheld this principle even at immense personal cost. One such occasion was when, in Adrianople, on the eve of His imprisonment in the fortress of 'Akká, a number of foreign diplomats begged Him to flee and offered Him asylum in their own countries. Spurning their advice, He submitted to the imperial edict, knowing all too well that 'Akká was worse, in many respects, than the notorious "Black Pit" of Tehran. Long afterward, when the governor of 'Akká (who by this time had entrusted his own son to Bahá'u'lláh's family for education and moral guidance) urged Him to leave the prison and offered to take full responsibility, He still refused, pointing out that such action would be contrary to the sultan's decree. Though Bahá'u'lláh deeply loved the beauty of the countryside, and His confinement deprived Him of seeing so much as a blade of grass, He voluntarily remained a prisoner for years after the original sentence had become a dead letter. He was finally persuaded to leave only in the sunset of His life, after it had become obvious that neither the sultan (a new one, by this time) nor anyone else in authority objected to His doing so.

Bahá'u'lláh spent His last years in the country mansion of Bahjí in 'Akká, surrounded by the scenic beauty He cherished. By this time the Bahá'í Faith had grown considerably and the body of the believers had placed substantial funds at His disposal. Even so, He maintained a lifestyle of extreme austerity, spending the money not on Himself but in promoting the Faith and helping the poor of 'Akká. So generous were Bahá'u'lláh and His family that they themselves often went without things that in other households would have been considered necessities. Thus He ended His career with the same solicitude for the needy that had marked its inception.

As mentioned previously, there were Muslim and Christian ecclesiastics who represented Bahá'u'lláh as a selfish charlatan. It would be grossly unfair, however, to imply that all clergy have shown hostility to the Bahá'í Faith and its founder. Theological differences aside, many have paid tribute to the purity and heroism of Bahá'u'lláh's life. One such was the Reverend T. K. Cheyne (mentioned earlier) who researched Bahá'u'lláh thoroughly and expressed his findings in *The Reconciliation of Races and Religions:*

"There was living quite lately a human being of such consummate excellence that many think it is both permissible and inevitable even to identify him mystically with the invisible Godhead. . . . If there has been any prophet in recent times, it is to Bahá'u'lláh that we must go. Character is the final judge. Bahá'u'lláh was a man of the highest class – that of prophets." (Appreciations 18)

A non-Bahá'í scholar, Alfred W. Martin, delivered an excellent summation in *Comparative Religion and the Religion of the Future.* He writes that since its inception the Bahá'í Faith

"has been identified with Bahá'u'lláh, who paid the price of prolonged exile, imprisonment, bodily suffering, and mental anguish for the faith He cherished – a man of imposing personality as revealed in His writings, characterized by intense moral earnestness and profound spirituality, gifted with the selfsame power so conspicuous in the character of Jesus, the power to appreciate people ideally, that is, to see them at the level of their best and to make even the lowest types think well of themselves because of potentialities within them to which He pointed, but of which they were wholly unaware; a prophet whose greatest contribution was not any specific doctrine He proclaimed, but an informing spiritual power breathed into the world through the example of His life and thereby quickening souls into new spiritual activity." (Appreciations 22-3)

What of the Báb and 'Abdu'l-Bahá? Space precludes any attempt to provide here even a sketchy outline of their lives, about which many fact-packed volumes have been written. What I will do, however, is quote the judgment of respected observers who were familiar with those lives and who cannot be accused of partiality, the more so because they were not Bahá'ís.

As to the Báb's moral character, independent historians have expressed remarkable agreement. "Who can fail to be attracted by the gentle spirit of [the Báb]?" writes E. G. Browne,

> *"His sorrowful and persecuted life; his purity of conduct, and youth; his courage and uncomplaining patience under misfortune . . . but most of all his tragic death, all serve to enlist our sympathies on behalf of the young Prophet of Shíráz. The irresistible charm which won him such devotion during his life still lives on. . . ."* (Browne, "The Bábís of Persia," *Journal of the Royal Asiatic Society* [1899], p. 933, quoted in DB 516n)

Sir Francis Younghusband writes:

> *"The story of the Báb . . . was the story of spiritual heroism unsurpassed. . . . The Báb's passionate sincerity could not be doubted, for he had given his life for his faith. And that there must be something in his message that appealed to men and satisfied their souls was witnessed to by the fact that thousands gave their lives in his cause and millions now follow him. If a young man could, in only six years of ministry, by the sincerity of his purpose and the attraction of his personality, so inspire rich and poor, cultured and illiterate . . . his life must be one of those events in the last hundred years which is really worth study."* (Younghusband, *The Gleam*, quoted in ibid. 516-17n)

A. L. M. Nicolas, the prominent French historian who meticulously researched the episode of the Báb, writes:

> *"His life is one of the most magnificent examples of courage which it has been the privilege of mankind to behold. . . . He sacrificed himself for humanity, for it he gave his body and his soul, for it he endured privations, insults, torture and martyrdom. He sealed, with his very lifeblood, the covenant of universal brotherhood. Like Jesus he paid with his life for the proclamation of a reign of concord, equity and brotherly love. More than anyone he knew what dreadful dangers he was heaping*

upon himself . . . but all these considerations could not weaken his resolve. Fear had no hold upon his soul and, perfectly calm, never looking back, in full possession of his powers, he walked into the furnace." (Nicolas, *Siyyid 'Alí-Muhammad*, quoted in ibid. 515n)

'Abdu'l-Bahá, Who was more accessible to Western observers than either the Báb or Bahá'u'lláh, was the object of many similar testimonies. Rather than quote several short impressions, I have decided to reprint one moderately long one by Myron H. Phelps, a prominent New York attorney who was not a Bahá'í but who visited 'Akká in December 1902. Phelps recorded his experiences and observations in a book about 'Abdu'l-Bahá entitled *Life and Teachings of Abbas Effendi*. One passage describes a typical gathering of the Palestinian poor – "a crowd of human beings with patched and tattered garments." Phelps continues:

"It is a noteworthy gathering. Many of these men are blind; many more are pale, emaciated, or aged. . . . Most of the women are closely veiled, but enough are uncovered to cause us well to believe that, if the veils were lifted, more pain and misery would be seen. Some of them carry babes with pinched and sallow faces. There are perhaps a hundred in this gathering, and besides, many children. They are of all the races one meets in these streets – Syrians, Arabs, Ethiopians, and many others.

"These people are ranged against the walls or seated on the ground, apparently in an attitude of expectation; – for what do they wait? Let us wait with them.

"We have not long to wait. A door opens and a man comes out. He is of middle stature, strongly built. He wears flowing light-colored robes. On his head is a light buff fez with a white cloth wound about it. He is perhaps sixty years of age. His long grey hair rests on his shoulders. His forehead is broad, full, and high, his nose slightly aquiline, his moustaches and beard, the latter full though not heavy, nearly white. His eyes are grey and blue, large, and both soft and penetrating. His bearing is simple, but there is grace, dignity, and even majesty about his movements. He passes through the crowd, and as he goes utters words of salutation. We do not understand them, but we see the benignity and the kindliness of his countenance. He stations himself at a narrow angle of the street and motions to the people to come towards him. They crowd up a little too insistently. He pushes them gently back and lets them pass him one by one. As they come they hold their hands extended. In each

open palm he places some small coins. * *He knows them all. He caresses them with his hand on the face, on the shoulders, on the head. Some he stops and questions. An aged negro who hobbles up, he greets with some kindly inquiry; the old man's broad face breaks into a sunny smile, his white teeth glistening against his ebony skin as he replies. He stops a woman with a babe and fondly strokes the child. As they pass, some kiss his hand. To all he says, 'Marhabbah, marhabbah' – 'Well done, well done!'*

"So they all pass him. The children have been crowding around him with extended hands, but to them he has not given. However, at the end, as he turns to go, he throws a handful of coppers over his shoulder, for which they scramble.

"During this time this friend of the poor has not been unattended. Several men wearing red fezes, and with earnest and kindly faces, followed him from the house, stood near him and aided in regulating the crowd, and now, with reverent manner and at a respectful distance, follow him away. When they address him they call him 'Master.'

"This scene you may see almost any day of the year in the streets of 'Akká. There are other scenes like it, which come only at the beginning of the winter season. In the cold weather which is approaching, the poor will suffer, for, as in all cities, they are thinly clad. Some day at this season, if you are advised of the place and time, you may see the poor of 'Akká gathered at one of the shops where clothes are sold, receiving cloaks from the Master. Upon many, especially the most infirm or crippled, he himself places the garment, adjusts it with his own hands, and strokes it approvingly, as if to say, 'There! Now you will do well.' There are five or six hundred poor in 'Akká, to all of whom he gives a warm garment each year.

"On feast days he visits the poor at their homes. He chats with them, inquires into their health and comfort, mentions by name those who are absent, and leaves gifts for all.

"Nor is it the beggars only that he remembers. Those respectable poor who cannot beg, but must suffer in silence – those whose daily labor will not support their families – to these he sends bread secretly. His left hand knoweth not what his right hand doeth.

---

*Describing a similar occasion, Corinne True points out that 'Abdu'l-Bahá's charity was reserved for the truly needy: ". . . once in a while we would see Him send someone away empty-handed and He would reprimand him for his laziness." (quoted in Honnold, *Vignettes* 80.)

"All the people know him and love him – the rich and the poor, the young and the old – even the babe leaping in its mother's arms. If he hears of any one sick in the city – [Muslim] or Christian, or of any other sect, it matters not – he is each day at their bedside, or sends a trusty messenger. If a physician is needed, and the patient poor, he brings or sends one, and also the necessary medicine. If he finds a leaking roof or a broken window menacing health, he summons a workman, and waits himself to see the breach repaired. If any one is in trouble – if a son or a brother is thrown into prison, or he is threatened at law, or falls into any difficulty too heavy for him – it is to the Master that he straightway makes appeal for counsel or for aid. Indeed, for counsel all come to him, rich as well as poor. He is the kind father of all the people. . . .

"For more than thirty-four years this man has been a prisoner at 'Akká. But his jailors have become his friends. The Governor of the city, the Commander of the Army Corps, respect and honor him as though he were their brother. No man's opinion or recommendation has greater weight with them. He is the beloved of all the city, high and low. And how could it be otherwise? For to this man it is the law, as it was to Jesus of Nazareth, to do good to those who injure him. Have we yet heard of any one in lands which boast the name of Christ who lived that life?

"Hear how he treats his enemies. One instance of many I have heard will suffice.

"When the Master came to 'Akká there lived there a certain man from Afghanistan, an austere and rigid [Muslim]. To him the Master was a heretic. He felt and nourished a great enmity towards the Master, and roused up others against him. When opportunity offered in gatherings of the people, as in the Mosque, he denounced him with bitter words.

"'This man,' he said to all, 'is an imposter. Why do you speak to him? Why do you have dealings with him?' And when he passed the Master on the street he was careful to hold his robe before his face that his sight might not be defiled.

"Thus did the Afghan. The Master, however, did thus: The Afghan was poor and lived in a mosque; he was frequently in need of food and clothing. The Master sent him both. These he accepted, but without thanks. He fell sick. The Master took him a physician, food, medicine, money. These, also, he accepted; but as he held out one hand that the physician might take his pulse, with the other he held his cloak before his face that he might not look upon the Master. For twenty-four years the Master continued his kindnesses and the Afghan persisted in his

enmity. Then at last one day the Afghan came to the Master's door, and fell down, penitent and weeping, at his feet.
"'Forgive me, sir!' he cried. 'For twenty-four years I have done evil to you, for twenty-four years you have done good to me. Now I know that I have been in the wrong.'
"The Master bade him rise, and they became friends.
"The Master is as simple as his soul is great. He claims nothing for himself – neither comfort, nor honor, nor repose. Three or four hours of sleep suffice him; all the remainder of his time and all his strength are given to the succour of those who suffer, in spirit or in body. 'I am,' he says, 'the servant of God.'
"Such is 'Abbás Effendi, the Master of 'Akká." (Phelps, *Life and Teachings* 2-10)

We must remember that apart from His ceaseless charitable labors, 'Abdu'l-Bahá devoted hours of each day to writing letters, holding meetings, giving talks, directing the far-flung affairs of the Faith, constructing – often with His own hands – the Shrine of the Báb, and developing a detailed plan of expansion destined to carry the Bahá'í Faith into the twenty-first century and beyond. When World War I broke out, it was He Who launched medical and agricultural relief projects in Palestine, preventing mass starvation – a service for which He later received a title He never used: Sir 'Abdu'l-Bahá 'Abbás, Knight of the British Empire. As the war drew to a close, Haifa remained in the hands of Turks who vowed to crucify 'Abdu'l-Bahá and all His family on Mount Carmel. When General Allenby's British forces swept into the region, the general went first for counsel to the Master, then cabled his astonished superiors in London: "Have today taken Palestine. Notify the world that 'Abdu'l-Bahá is safe." (Blomfield, *Chosen Highway* 220)

'Abdu'l-Bahá was a man Who would – and often did, literally – give one the shirt off His back. Many a time He took aside some needy passerby or street urchin, bestowing upon that astonished person some garment He had on: robe, cloak, coat, occasionally even trousers. As He lay dying in 1921, His daughter sought to change His nightshirt, only to discover He was wearing the only one He had – the others He had all given away. His funeral brought together, in a vivid and united experience of grief, what almost certainly was the largest-ever public gathering of Haifa's many religious, ethnic, and cultural communities.

To present someone's character through selected highlights and personal impressions is unsatisfactory at best. It risks being unfair, both to the reader and to the person thus presented. The vignettes I have offered are intended primarily to whet curiosity and spur independent research. Any inquirer will find at his or her disposal a great deal of well-documented biographical material on the lives of the Central Figures of the Bahá'í Faith. A world-renowned expert on character once said: "Ye shall know them by their fruits. Do men gather grapes of thorns, or figs of thistles?" (Matt. 7:16) My conviction that the Báb, Bahá'u'lláh, and 'Abdu'l-Bahá lived lives of towering, almost unheard-of goodness and nobility might not by itself cause me to conclude that They were channels of divine authority. Without such conviction as a catalyst, however, I would remain unmoved by any purely logical clues or indications such as prophecies, scientific revelations, innate knowledge, spellbinding personal magnetism, and the like. One whose heart is touched by the beauty of these men's lives, and who not only understands but feels Their never-failing harmony of word and action – only such a person, I would wager, will be inclined to take seriously any other evidence of inspiration, however compelling or tantalizing it might appear.

THE DIVINE WORD

This chapter has focused, until now, on Bahá'u'lláh's teaching that the Manifestation of God is His own proof. We have explored two potentially useful ways of understanding this statement: first, that the Manifestation should make a uniquely powerful impression on those who encounter Him, and second, that He must distinguish Himself by peerless character and iron consistency. Bahá'u'lláh admirably fulfilled both expectations.

In His writings, however, Bahá'u'lláh carries this idea a step further. He states that just as the Manifestation is His own proof to those who know Him, so is His revealed word – the Word of God – its own proof to those who read and reflect upon it. This intriguing concept warrants close attention. Of all the evidence Bahá'u'lláh offers, His own written word is the one to which we have the most immediate access. It is something we can experience directly without need to rely on data compiled by historians, biographers, scientists, literary scholars, and the like. What, then, does He mean when He says the revealed word is its own proof?

His meaning, as I have come to understand it, is this: The words that descend upon the Messenger of God through divine revelation are distinguished from human writing by certain characteristics – characteristics that we as human beings can discern but can never reproduce or emulate. The proof of the divine word is our inability to create anything like it. "No breeze," He says, "can compare with the breezes of Divine Revelation, whilst the Word which is uttered by God shineth and flasheth as the sun amidst the books of men. Happy the man that hath discovered it, and recognized it. . . ." (ESW 42-3) He states:

> *"He, the divine King, hath proclaimed the undisputed supremacy of the verses of His book over all things that testify to His truth. For compared with all other proofs and tokens, the divinely-revealed verses shine as the sun, whilst all others are as stars. To the peoples of the world they are the abiding testimony, the incontrovertible proof, the shining light of the ideal King. Their excellence is unrivaled, their virtue nothing can surpass. They are the treasury of the divine pearls and the depository of the divine mysteries. . . . Through them floweth the river of divine knowledge, and gloweth the fire of His ancient and consummate wisdom."* (KI 204)

What are the specific qualities of revealed writing that no human author can replicate? Bahá'u'lláh identifies two characteristics that set apart the Word of God from the words of men: (1) its creative power to stimulate spiritual growth – a power different both in degree and in kind from anything else in existence; and (2) its limitless depth of meaning.

The Creative Power

The Word of God, according to Bahá'u'lláh, is the outward form of an inward reality – the mysterious spiritual energy released into the world when God speaks through His Manifestation. This celestial force, channeled through the Manifestation and expressed through His speech, shares with the Manifestation Himself the distinction of reflecting perfectly all the attributes of God such as knowledge, love, justice, dominion, and an infinity of others.

We have previously discussed what Bahá'u'lláh says about the indirect influence of revelation – the spiritual energy diffused throughout the world when God reveals Himself. It is not, however, with such an indirect effect that we are here concerned. We are interested rather in the creative power by which, Bahá'u'lláh says, the Word acts directly upon those who turn towards it and open themselves to its influence:

> *"Intone, O My servant, the verses of God that have been received by thee, as intoned by them who have drawn nigh unto Him, that the sweetness of thy melody may kindle thine own soul, and attract the hearts of all men. Whoso reciteth, in the privacy of his chamber, the verses revealed by God, the scattering angels of the Almighty shall scatter*

abroad the fragrance of the words uttered by his mouth, and shall cause the heart of every righteous man to throb. Though he may, at first, remain unaware of its effect, yet the virtue of the grace vouchsafed unto him must needs sooner or later exercise its influence upon his soul. Thus have the mysteries of the Revelation of God been decreed by virtue of the Will of Him Who is the Source of power and wisdom." (G 295)

Such claims are not, of course, confined to the revelation of Bahá'u'lláh. In the Old Testament, God says:

"For as the rain cometh down, and the snow from heaven, and returneth not thither, but watereth the earth, and maketh it bring forth and bud, that it may give seed to the sower, and bread to the eater: So shall my word be that goeth forth out of my mouth: it shall not return unto me void, but it shall accomplish that which I please, and it shall prosper in the thing whereto I sent it." (Isa. 55:10-11)

Jesus put it simply: "The words that I speak unto you, they are spirit, and they are life." (John 6:63) Bahá'u'lláh likens the divine word to "bread from heaven," "life-giving water," and sunlight that causes the seed of the human heart to germinate and grow. Of its influence on individual growth He says:

"Through the Teachings of this Day Star of Truth every man will advance and develop until he attaineth the station at which he can manifest all the potential forces with which his inmost true self hath been endowed." (G 68)

Now let us consider the second distinguishing attribute of the Divine Word:

The Hidden Mysteries
According to Bahá'u'lláh, the Word of God is the storehouse not only of infinite creative power but of infinite meaning: "Know assuredly . . . that its meaning can never be exhausted." (G 175) Each of the revealed utterances, He teaches, can be understood on countless levels, and within each level there are unnumbered implications – some veiled, others obvious.
In His own commentaries on other scripture, Bahá'u'lláh often returns to this theme. Regarding a Gospel passage, He writes: "This servant will now share with thee a dewdrop out of the fathomless ocean of the truths treasured in these holy words." (KI 28) He then spends many pages unfolding the author's purpose and intent. Of a similar verse from the Qur'án He says:

"Were We to expound its inner meanings and unfold its hidden mysteries, eternity would never suffice to exhaust their import, nor would the universe be capable of hearing them!" (ibid. 204) Finally, concerning His own words He makes this astounding assertion:

> *"My holy, My divinely ordained Revelation may be likened unto an ocean in whose depths are concealed innumerable pearls of great price, of surpassing luster. It is the duty of every seeker to bestir himself and strive to attain the shores of this ocean, so that he may, in proportion to the eagerness of his search and the efforts he hath exerted, partake of such benefits as have been pre-ordained in God's irrevocable and hidden Tablets."* (G 326)

Nor is any seeker restricted to the "shores of this ocean," for Bahá'u'lláh writes elsewhere: "Immerse yourselves in the ocean of My words, that ye may unravel its secrets, and discover all the pearls of wisdom that lie hid in its depths." (ibid. 136)

Diving into the Divine Ocean

When we dive for pearls in a literal ocean, we gain more than pearls: We experience the force and beauty of the ocean itself. So it is when we dive for "pearls of wisdom" in the symbolic ocean of revelation – "the Ocean Whose waters refresh, by virtue of the Will of God, the souls of men" (G 294). By searching out the deeper meanings and hidden implications of Bahá'u'lláh's writings, we experience directly their vitalizing power. We can never do this merely by skimming the surface – a point Bahá'u'lláh makes succinctly in the following prayer:

> *"Number me not with them who read Thy words and fail to find Thy hidden gift which, as decreed by Thee, is contained therein, and which quickeneth the souls of Thy creatures and the hearts of Thy servants."* (PM 83)

What does this mean, in practical terms, to an inquirer who seeks to determine whether the words of Bahá'u'lláh are divine or human in origin? Simply this: Plunge into a personal study of His writings! Do not rely on the opinions, interpretations, or commentaries of others: Go directly to the source. Read Bahá'u'lláh with an open mind and an open heart; delve below the surface to determine whether His words really do contain "hidden pearls" of meaning and implication. If they seem to do so, then explore and reflect upon those deeper meanings. This in no way implies that one must start out by believing Bahá'u'lláh is Who He claims to be; the goal, after all, is to find out. Nor does it mean that an uncommitted reader must necessarily agree with everything that Bahá'u'lláh says. If, at some point, one comes to believe in Bahá'u'lláh's divine authority, then logically one must also believe in His teachings – but an investigator is under no such obligation. The point is not to agree but to understand and, in seeking that understanding, to put oneself in a position to experience spiritual transformation.

The late Dr. Daniel C. Jordan, a Bahá'í who was a psychologist and educator, analyzes this process of transformation in a groundbreaking paper entitled "Becoming Your True Self". He makes one particularly crucial point:

"Personal transformation is a fundamental reason that people are attracted to the Faith, develop conviction as to its truth, and finally become Bahá'ís. The reason is simple. People who come in contact with the Faith and feel themselves being transformed by it have an experience that is self-validating. No one can take that experience away from them and no intellectual argument can make it appear insignificant or unreal. Feeling oneself becoming the best of what one can potentially be constitutes the highest joy. It promotes a sense of self-worth, obviates the need for expressing hostility, and guarantees a compassionate social conscience – all prerequisites of world unity and peace." (Jordan, *Becoming Your True Self* 4)

Immersing ourselves in the "ocean" of Bahá'u'lláh's writings is easy but not necessarily effortless. Bahá'u'lláh, as quoted earlier, states that the benefits one derives will be "in proportion to the eagerness of his search and the efforts he hath exerted." For Bahá'ís, the study of their sacred texts is a lifetime endeavor; it requires, among other things, willingness to entertain new ideas and to relinquish cherished prejudices and misconceptions as their understanding grows. Shoghi Effendi writes: "The more we read the Writings, the more truths we can find in them, the more will see that our previous notions were erroneous." (LG 313)

How one proceeds will necessarily depend on one's interests and spiritual orientation. One who believes in God, for example, and who feels inclined to turn towards Him in prayer, may try using Bahá'u'lláh's written prayers in his or her personal devotions. There are several translated volumes of such prayers, covering every imaginable need and topic – prayers for insight, for spiritual development, for aid and assistance, for praise and thanksgiving, for special occasions, for friends and family, and for innumerable other purposes. (Bahá'ís can and do pray in their own words, but they believe the prayers of Bahá'u'lláh, being divinely revealed, have a special potency that no human speech can match.) An agnostic or atheist will probably take a different approach (since one may well feel hypocritical speaking to a being in whom one does not believe). Such an approach might consist simply of meditating on Bahá'u'lláh's writings. Bahá'u'lláh Himself states that "One hour's reflection is preferable to seventy years of pious worship." (KI 238)

One may choose a specific theme – life after death, world peace, the nature of God, or any other subject in which one takes an interest – and explore what Bahá'u'lláh says about it, pulling together His statements from various places in various books. Often, in this way, one will gain some sudden insight by realizing that a seemingly unrelated statement actually has a direct bearing on the matter. Or one may take a specific book by Bahá'u'lláh and study it from beginning to end – perhaps His *Book of Certitude*, in which He explores the symbolic meaning of age-old prophecy; or His *Hidden Words*, which sets forth the essentials of good character and spiritual development; or His *Seven Valleys*, in which He defines true mysticism; or His *Epistle to the Son of the Wolf*, in which He reminisces about His own life and presents a mini-anthology of His earlier writings. There are many others, including compilations of His most important letters and essays. The approach is less important than the effort, for Bahá'u'lláh promises divine assistance to anyone who sincerely tries to uncover the truth: "Whoso maketh efforts for Us," He says, quoting the Qur'án, "in Our ways shall We assuredly guide him." (KI 195)

If Bahá'u'lláh is really the Voice of God, then by undertaking such an experiment open-mindedly and with reasonable patience, we should soon enough sense the superhuman power and potency with which He claims His words are charged: "Though he may, at first, remain unaware of its effect, yet the virtue of the grace vouchsafed unto him must sooner or later exercise its influence upon his soul." (G 295) By putting this promise to the test, we gain the most direct and important evidence imaginable in our quest.

The Bahá'í Community

While personal exposure and introspection are the best ways to test the creative power of any purported revelation, they are not the only ways. We must expect any phenomenon so remarkable to have social consequences that we can investigate empirically. "Such," says Bahá'u'lláh, "is the binding force of the Word of God, which uniteth the hearts of them that have renounced all else but Him. . . ." (KI 112)

This statement may surprise some people. There is an opinion, fashionable in some circles, that religion is the world's primary cause of war, disunity, and intolerance; that all human progress is achieved not because of, but in spite of, religion; and that society really would be better off without it. Whenever religion does cease to bring about love and unity, Bahá'ís would agree that its absence is preferable, for they believe the primary purpose of religion is the promotion of love and unity. Does it do this – or are the cynics correct in arguing that it does the opposite?

A Bahá'í would reply that religion serves its unifying purpose so long as its adherents remain true to the vision and spirit of the Manifestation of God Who revealed it. True religion is more than stately buildings; it is more than formal creeds and ceremonies; it is more than choirs, or stained glass, or any of the other outward trappings we may associate with it. These things are neither wrong nor harmful in themselves, but they are not what religion is about. "The essence of religion," says Bahá'u'lláh, "is to testify unto that which the Lord hath revealed, and follow that which He hath ordained in His mighty Book." (TB 155) If we disregard religious institutions and look instead at the historical effects of the world's holy books, what do we see?

We see, with unmistakable clarity, that those books collectively have provided the most powerful unifying, civilizing force in human history. Every world faith has begun in darkest obscurity with the teachings of some lone individual – a Christ, a Buddha, a Muḥammad – Who claimed to be the mouthpiece of an invisible Supreme Intelligence. In each case the teachings of the founder were compiled into a book that became the rallying point for the religious community. Each religion grew slowly, usually over a period of centuries, and always against violent resistance, to establish itself as a major force in society. Each one, in doing so, brought under its umbrella hundreds of formerly hostile tribes, nationalities, cults, and cultures, infusing into its members a higher loyalty and a spirit of brotherhood under one God. This unifying impulse, on each such occasion, has brought into being a new civilization more advanced than any that previously had appeared.

This recurring cycle is more than a mere fact of history. It is the central, most significant fact of history. Unfortunately, every cycle has a down side as well as an up side. The down side is that humankind eventually loses touch with the pure teachings of the religion's founder. Prophetic enthusiasm gives way to custom and complacency. Then crusades and inquisitions are launched in the name of Christ, Who commanded His followers to turn the other cheek (Matt. 5:39) and "Put up again thy sword into his place." (Matt. 26:52) Then holy wars are waged in the name of Muḥammad, Who used force only in self-defense, and Who said: "Let there be no compulsion in religion." (Q 2:257) Then it becomes easy for intellectuals, seeing religion in its decay, to condemn it as a source of hatred and fanaticism.

This is why, Bahá'ís believe, religion must be periodically renewed. This renewal cannot be accomplished by ecumenical movements that reach into the past in an effort to recapture the pristine purity of their faith. It can only be renewed by God, speaking through a new Messenger, adapting His laws to the new age, and providing new teachings in accordance with humanity's readiness.

Whatever our feelings about religion, we can hardly deny that the most influential books in history have been the world's great religious scriptures – the Bhagavad-Gita, the Upanishads, the Zend-Avesta, the Bible, the Qur'án. These, to an incomparably greater extent than the works of any secular writer or philosopher, have shaped the course of civilization; they have also uplifted thousands of millions of individual lives. As the Bahá'í writer Marzieh Gail once expressed it, "How many homes have ever had an Old Family Aristotle?" Viewing the matter in this way, we see why Bahá'u'lláh would say "The Word of God is the king of words and its pervasive influence is incalculable. It hath ever dominated and will continue to dominate the realm of being." (TB 173)

I have suggested that if Bahá'u'lláh's words are genuine revelation, the creative force they embody can be expected to have observable social consequences. The implications of this point should now be a bit clearer. If Bahá'u'lláh is Who He claims to be, then the emerging worldwide Bahá'í community is actually the embryo of a new civilization, just as the early Jewish, Christian, or Muslim communities, at comparable stages of development, were embryonic civilizations. In that case it should display a dynamic cohesiveness, an evolutionary vigor contrasting starkly with the social disintegration prevalent in today's world. Such a phenomenon might not be obvious to a casual observer: Arnold Toynbee remarks in *A Study of History* that the Christian Faith, in the Hellenizing world of the second century, loomed no larger than the Bahá'í Faith does in the Westernizing world of today. (Toynbee, *Study of History*, vol. VIII, p. 117) Still, the signs of such a development, if they exist, should be visible to anyone who consciously looks for them.

Those signs abound. The relative newness and smallness of the Bahá'í Faith serve to render all the more amazing two of its most striking characteristics: its human diversity and its geographical spread.

As to its diversity, the various races, tribes, nationalities, and religious and ethnic backgrounds represented within the Bahá'í community number in the thousands, while the community's continuing expansion leaves all official statistics obsolete long before they can be published. Every attempted membership breakdown runs to many pages of fine print; when we scan those pages, we usually find every human subgroup we have ever heard of, plus countless others we have not.

Marcus Bach, former professor of comparative religion at the University of Iowa, verified this diversity in his travels:

> *"Wherever I have gone to research the faith called Bahá'í, I have been astonished at what I have found. . . . I am continually intrigued by the Bahá'í people . . . representing the basic cultural and ethnic groups around the world and embracing obscure and little-known localities in far-flung lands where even Christianity has barely gone. . . . I have met them in the most unexpected places, in a war-torn village in southeast Asia, in African cities, in industrial Mexico, in the executive branches of big industry in Iran, in schools and colleges on foreign campuses, in American cities and villages, wherever people dream of the age-old concept of the brotherhood of man and the fatherhood of God . . . the Bahá'ís are there."* (Bach, *Strangers* 75-6)

As Bach suggests, the Bahá'í commitment to diversity goes far beyond membership statistics: It transforms the personal lives of its adherents. Long before the civil rights movement in the American South or the dismantling of apartheid in South Africa, Bahá'í communities in those places were actively practicing racial integration and intermarriage. The Bahá'í Faith has brought together Brahmins and untouchables in caste-conscious India, Protestants and Catholics in strife-torn northern Ireland, Jews and Arabs in the Middle East. Robert Semple, a member of the Management Committee of the Presbyterian Church, is among many to make such comments as these:

> *". . . nor can one wonder at the rapid growth in Christian Countries of the new Bahá'í World Faith, which is also gaining many adherents among the people of Asia and Africa; for that Faith has as its motive power a burning belief in the Fatherhood of God, the brotherhood of men, of all creeds and races, and, here is the point, like the early Christian Church, it practices what it preaches."* (Semple, *British Weekly,* 26 August 1954, quoted in Winston Evans and Marzieh Gail, "The Voice from Inner Space," *World Order,* Summer 1967, p. 40)

Closely linked to this diversity is the astonishing geographical distribution of the international Bahá'í community. The *Encyclopaedia Britannica,* in its 1988 Yearbook and subsequent annual editions, published a table of comparative statistics for each of the important world religions. While the Bahá'í Faith was among the smallest of these numerically, *Britannica* ranked it as second only to Christianity in the number of countries where it has a "significant following."

In addition to human diversity and geographical spread, the worldwide Bahá'í community displays several other features that testify to the creative power of Bahá'u'lláh's revealed words. Among these is the indivisible unity of the Administrative Order through which Bahá'ís, wherever they reside, conduct and coordinate their activities. To the best of my knowledge, no other widespread, highly diversified religious movement has ever survived for more than a century without dividing into sects and factions.

Organizational unity, however, is simply a vessel for the far more important sense of spiritual fellowship that animates believers. Consider the effect of the Bahá'í belief in progressive revelation. Followers of any and all faiths – Jewish, Buddhist, Muslim, Christian, Hindu, or Zoroastrian – who rally around Bahá'u'lláh do so without sacrificing their spiritual roots. Bahá'ís of Christian background, for example, revere Jesus and the Bible no less than persons who consider themselves Christian in an exclusive sense. To accept Bahá'u'lláh as the spiritual reappearance of Christ is not to deny Christ; it is to follow Him in His Second Coming. Likewise, Bahá'ís of Buddhist origin need not abandon Buddha; those of Muslim background do not desert Muḥammad; and so forth. By accepting Bahá'u'lláh as the Promised One of *all* religions, devotees of diverse faiths find common ground while strengthening and clarifying their traditional beliefs. The result is a vibrant bond of brotherhood that no eclectic or ecumenical movement can duplicate.

A further sign of the community's cohesive vitality is its shared sense of history. Bahá'í historian Douglas Martin expresses the Faith's pride in a legacy that includes, among other things, twenty thousand early martyrs:

> *"Apart from its lively interest in the spiritual giants of earlier Revelations it has its own archetypal heroes and saints (for whom its children are named) whose lives provide moral example and whose spiritual achievements have already begun to evoke the first halting response of Bahá'í artists, writers, and musicians. Today, all around the world, an entire generation of Japanese, Italian, Bolivian, Ugandan, Canadian and Persian children are being educated in this common tradition."*
> (Martin, "Bahá'u'lláh's Model for World Fellowship", *World Order*, Fall 1976, pp. 16-7)

Together they are learning, for instance, the story of the mother of Ashraf, a young Persian Bahá'í. The mother was seated in a room with Ashraf's teenage wife when the two women heard an approaching mob chanting anti-Bahá'í hate slogans. Before either could react, someone in the crowd hurled into the room the severed head of Ashraf; whereupon the young bride fainted. The mother, however, calmly washed the blood from her son's head, then threw it back to the crowd with words now cherished by Bahá'ís everywhere: "What we have given to God we do not take back!"

Still another remarkable feature of Bahá'í community life is its effectiveness as a catalyst for harmonious social change. Bahá'í groups and individuals, working at the grassroots level in thousands of localities throughout the planet, are translating Bahá'u'lláh's universal ideals into practical programs of social and economic development. Their achievements have won, and are increasingly winning, not only the admiration but the active support of public and private agencies with which they coordinate their humanitarian efforts.

Combined with its astonishing diversity and its geographical spread, these characteristics – administrative and spiritual unity, a shared sense of history, and a demonstrated commitment to social change – invest the Bahá'í community with a pulsating evolutionary vigor that one must experience to understand. Having experienced it, we are free to explain it in any way we like; what we cannot do is ignore it or deny its reality.

The springboard for this discussion was Bahá'u'lláh's teaching that the revealed Word of God is its own proof by virtue of its inimitable qualities – one of these being the power to bring into being a new civilization. This audacious statement has led us to ask what facts, if any, support the Faith's vision of itself as the nucleus and prototype of a burgeoning world order. Is it reasonable, given conditions within the emerging Bahá'í community, to interpret its existence and momentum as deriving from the same spiritual impulse that produced the great religions and civilizations of the past?

There is, of course, no mathematically rigorous way to answer such a question; sociology is anything but an exact science. But however we interpret these signs, they testify to the awe-inspiring influence that Bahá'u'-lláh's words have already exerted, and continue to exert, in the lives of an ever-swelling portion of humanity. Shoghi Effendi sums up the situation:

"The Faith of Bahá'u'lláh has assimilated, by virtue of its creative, its regulative and ennobling energies, the varied races, nationalities, creeds and classes that have sought its shadow, and have pledged unswerving fealty to its cause. It has changed the hearts of its adherents, burned away their prejudices, stilled their passions, exalted their conceptions,

105

ennobled their motives, coordinated their efforts, and transformed their outlook. While preserving their patriotism and safeguarding their lesser loyalties, it has made them lovers of mankind. . . . While maintaining intact their belief in the Divine origin of their respective religions, it has enabled them to visualize the underlying purpose of these religions, to discover their merits, to recognize their sequence, their interdependence, their wholeness and unity. . . .

". . . this world-enfolding System, this many-hued and firmly-knit Fraternity, infus[es] into every man and woman it has won to its cause a faith, a hope, and a vigor that a wayward generation has long lost, and is powerless to recover. They who preside over the immediate destinies of this troubled world, they who are responsible for its chaotic state, its fears, its doubts, its miseries will do well, in their bewilderment, to fix their gaze and ponder in their hearts upon the evidences of this saving grace of the Almighty that lies within their reach – a grace that can ease their burden, resolve their perplexities, and illuminate their path." (WOB 197-201)

Chapter Seven
THE BOOK OF GOD IS OPEN

Extraordinary claims require extraordinary evidence.
—Carl Sagan

O ye that judge with fairness! If this Cause is to be denied then what other cause in this world can be vindicated or deemed worthy of acceptance?
—Bahá'u'lláh

NO ONE, AS THE INTRODUCTION to this book emphasizes, ever followed a religion purely on the basis of rational evidence. Nor should anyone ever do so. If one's heart does not respond to the Prophet's message with a certainty that goes beyond words and logic, if it does not ring true in the very core of one's being, then it is neither wise nor rational to believe.

Just the same, we have at least two compelling reasons to acquaint ourselves with the logical basis for religious faith. First, as 'Abdu'l-Bahá explains, "arguments are a guide to the path and by this the heart will be turned unto the Sun of Truth. And when the heart is turned unto the Sun, then the eye will be opened and will recognize the Sun through the Sun itself." (BWF 383-4) Second, even after one gains assurance, reason can support and clarify one's intuitive conviction. 'Abdu'l-Bahá encourages everyone to "exercise reason, analyze and logically examine the facts presented so that confidence will be inspired and faith attained" (PUP 327), to "acquire certainty of knowledge" concerning God and His Manifestations "through proofs and evidences and not through susceptibilities" (ibid. 227).

It is therefore necessary to investigate religion just as we would investigate any other aspect of reality. Shoghi Effendi states that the Bahá'í Faith is "scientific in its method" (*Selected Writings* 7) (referring, I assume, to its method of investigating truth, since that is the entire purpose of the scientific method, and since independent investigation of truth is the Faith's "first principle").

The scientific method may sound daunting to a nonscientist, but it need not be. It is nothing more than organized common sense. Harking back to chapter 3, we may define scientific method as the *testing* of a proposed *explanation* (or "hypothesis") by means of *data* derived from *experience*. In gathering such data and testing such explanations, one can and should apply every legitimate human faculty – observation, reason, intuition, and validated authority. The process must be potentially *public*; that is, based on data that can be verified, and procedures that can be successfully repeated, by any qualified investigator.

Any set of facts – however large – can be explained in more than one way. This means one can never really "prove" any useful scientific hypothesis. What scientists do, therefore, is to sneak up on an idea from behind: They try by every means at their disposal to disprove it. Each time a hypothesis survives a test that might have disproved it (or at least called it into question), the likelihood grows that it is true, and one's confidence in it increases. When an explanation consistently passes a large number of tests from many different directions, ties together a wide range of observations that previously seemed unrelated, correctly predicts new and unexpected findings, and accounts for a maximum of data with a minimum of complexity, we may rationally embrace that explanation as true (subject always to further testing).

This description is light-years away from popular stereotypes of scientific method, which mistakenly assume that science is concerned only with "laboratory facts" leading to "absolute proof." Any good scientist would scoff at such a notion. In science, as in law, one may hope to prove a hypothesis "beyond a reasonable doubt," but one can never eliminate every vestige of theoretical uncertainty. Once we become accustomed to this idea, there is nothing necessarily unsettling about it. It can be refreshing and even comforting: On the one hand, it allows us to act on our convictions with a high degree of confidence; on the other, it reminds us, ever so gently, that we must always remain open to new ideas and evidence.

There exists a pervasive feeling among Western intellectuals – believers and skeptics alike – that religion is "beyond" science and scientific method. Followers of traditional faiths frequently maintain that religious knowledge is of a higher order than scientific knowledge and that submitting those beliefs to the methods of science would demean or degrade them. Skeptics uphold the distinction for a quite different reason: They feel the basic tenets of religion are either patently superstitious, or else so vague, so unclear in their implications, that no conceivable test could prove them false. This would mean, from a scientific standpoint, that such tenets also could never be proved true. Any statement so general that no possible observation could contradict it, so nebulous that no real-life experience could call it into question, is a statement we can never confirm or validate by scientific means. The best we can do is suspend judgment. Modern doubters would banish all spiritual or mystical thinking to this limbo.

The claim of Bahá'u'lláh presents a ringing challenge to both camps. He identifies Himself as the bearer of a modern-day revelation from God – as One Whose appearance is, moreover, the fulfillment of the promises and prophecies of all other religions. He states His case, however, in terms so specific, so rich with concrete and testable implications, that it is fully open to evaluation by the methods of modern science. He says, for example, that the successive "Manifestations of God" (founders of religion and civilization, of Whom He claims to be the latest) have certain invariable attributes: They are infallible; They are omniscient at will; They see the future; They understand even the hidden secrets of physical reality; They possess innate knowledge not learned or learnable in any school. Their powers and perfections make Them stand out like the sun from ordinary men; Their characters are flawless models of resolve and consistency, even under bitterest adversity; and Their words resonate with creative power – power sufficient to transform individuals and change the course of history. Born in the appalling darkness of nineteenth-century Persia, deprived of anything resembling even a modern elementary school education, Bahá'u'lláh wrote hundreds of works tackling head-on the most intractable problems of today's world – a world not one of His learned contemporaries even dimly visualized. He left, moreover, the legacy of His life, itself an open book of which unnumbered details are preserved and documented.

Today's people of learning can tell us astounding things: the internal structure of the smallest atom, the composition of the farthest star, the appearance of animals that lived eons before the first human being. They deduce these facts from the most insubstantial wisps of evidence: a phantom trail in a cloud chamber, a glimmer of light that traveled towards earth for thousands of millions of years, a handful of fossilized bone splinters. With Bahá'u'lláh, however, the evidence is not wispy; it is mountainous. Cannot the same scientific method used by these intrepid explorers of reality – a method capable of unlocking such marvelous secrets – tell us whether Bahá'u'lláh was Who and What He claimed to be?

This book argues that anyone who really wishes to do so can find out whether Bahá'u'lláh was telling the truth about His identity. It further argues that in a world pregnant with promise on the one hand and dissolving in chaos on the other, we cannot afford to skirt the issue: We need to know whether He really was a Messenger from God. The stakes are extraordinarily high. Moreover, this is an issue that confronts each individual human being. The so-called "leaders of thought," into whose hands humanity seems to entrust its collective conscience, have for well over a century refused to acknowledge or even consider the claim of Bahá'u'lláh – much less examine the supporting evidence He offers.

The Case for Bahá'u'lláh

Against this background, I have presented some of that evidence: The writings of Bahá'u'lláh (along with those of the Báb and 'Abdu'l-Bahá, which bear the stamp of His authority) are liberally sprinkled with prophecies. These prophecies are detailed and specific; they name names and give locations; most refer to an identifiable time frame of limited duration. They cover, according to Bahá'u'lláh Himself, "most of the things which have come to pass on this earth" in such wise that "No possibility is left for anyone either to turn aside or protest." (ESW 148-150) Most of them ran counter to the conventional wisdom of the time. All were published well in advance of the events to which they refer, giving skeptics every opportunity to show that Bahá'u'lláh was capable of making mistakes. Yet not one prophecy proved to be in error. The great majority of these have been spectacularly fulfilled, sometimes at the last possible moment and against seemingly insuperable odds. The fulfillment of the few remaining others seems to be materializing before our eyes.

Prophecies of a historical nature taken from the Bahá'í scriptures include: the unexpected defeat and downfall of Napoleon III, emperor of France; the defeat of Germany in two bloody wars, resulting in the "lamentations of Berlin"; the conspicuous success and stability of Queen Victoria's reign; the dismissal of 'Álí Páshá, prime minister of Turkey; the subsequent overthrow and assassination of his chief, Sultan 'Abdu'l-'Azíz; the dismantling of the Ottoman Empire and the extinction of the "outward splendor" of its capital, Constantinople; the fate of Persia's Náṣiri'd-Dín Sháh as an "object lesson for the world"; the restrictions imposed upon the Persian monarchy by that country's Constitutional Revolution; the precipitous decline in the fortunes and prestige of monarchy throughout the world; the steady erosion of political and social power wielded by ecclesiastical institutions; the extinction of the caliphate, which held a position in Sunní Islam similar to that of the papacy in Roman Catholicism; the spread of communism – the "Movement of the Left" – and its rise to world power; the subsequent collapse of that same movement as a direct result of its obsession with forced economic equality; the rise of Israel as a Jewish homeland; the persecution of Jews on the European continent, which materialized in the Nazi holocaust; America's violent racial struggles, which, as foretold, threatened the country's survival by polarizing it during the tensest moments of the Cold War; Bahá'u'lláh's own release from the prison of 'Akká and the pitching of His tent on Mount Carmel; the seizure and desecration in Baghdad of Bahá'u'lláh's house – a Bahá'í shrine – by Muslim fanatics; and the complete collapse of every attempt to create sects and factions within the Bahá'í Faith.

Bahá'í prophecies that anticipated scientific discoveries include: the explosive acceleration of scientific and technological progress; the discovery of atomic weaponry as a force capable of poisoning the earth's entire atmosphere; the transmutation of elements, a long-sought technology now known to be responsible for nuclear power and which, as foreseen by Bahá'u'lláh, has therefore brought humanity to the brink of catastrophe; the discovery that complex chemical elements evolve in nature from simpler ones; the recognition that planets are a universal consequence of normal star formation; space travel "with the rapidity of rising lightning," reaching out not only to other planets but "from the globe of the earth to the globe of the sun"; the realization that certain forms of cancer are communicable; the failure of all efforts to identify a "missing link" or common ancestor between man and ape; the collapse in physics of the theory of a mechanical ether and its replacement by an intellectual abstraction ("spacetime"); and the breakdown of mechanical models as a basis for understanding the physical world.

Other prophecies of Bahá'u'lláh and 'Abdu'l-Bahá seem intimately related to events taking place in the world today. These foretold, among other things, that a worldwide tide of oppression would be followed by a renaissance of liberty, leading ultimately to "unity in freedom"; that a "new world order" would emerge in which all nations, driven by "imperative necessity," would collectively resist aggression by any recalcitrant member; that these and other trends would lead ultimately to "the unity of nations – a unity which in this century will be firmly established, causing all the peoples of the world to regard themselves as citizens of one common fatherland"; the cataclysmic "rolling up" of the "present-day Order" as a prelude to world peace; the preponderating role to be played by America in the forging of that peace; the emergence of the Bahá'í Faith from obscurity and, as a temporary consequence, its repression in various parts of the world.

Bahá'u'lláh's seeming ability to peer into the future was not the only sign of His otherworldly knowledge. He spent His entire life in an atmosphere dominated by nineteenth-century Islamic fundamentalism, first in Persia, then as a prisoner of the Turks. He received only the most perfunctory tutoring, never went to school, never studied Western literature, indeed never experienced any outward influence that might plausibly have broadened His horizons or countered any of the deleterious effects of His early conditioning. Yet there is the startling modernity of His writing – a modernity that becomes more, rather than less, conspicuous every year as His social prescriptions appear increasingly relevant to world events, and which has evoked praise and appreciation from a host of independent observers. It was Bahá'u'lláh Who gave to the world its first comprehensive inventory of the spiritual and humanitarian principles that today constitute the essence of leading-edge thought. It was Bahá'u'lláh Who, long before such a concept had occurred to even His most advanced contemporaries, first described the world in detail as a global village and perceptively analyzed the problems it would face. He wrote with high eloquence and technical virtuosity not only in His native Persian, but also in Arabic – a language He never had any opportunity to study, yet which, according to scholars, cannot be mastered without years of arduous formal training. He composed His writings in both languages without premeditation, hesitation, or revision, dictating for hours at a time with such speed as to tax the most skilled stenographers. These spontaneous outpourings consistently display the very qualities one would expect of revelation: highly polished style, lucid organization, and exceptional literary force. At the same time, they exclude the lapses and inconsistencies typical of human extemporaneous rambling.

Bahá'u'lláh's personality and character were what one would logically expect of a Divine Manifestation. His personality was by all accounts so radiant, so majestic and magnetic as to lift Him high above the rank and file of humanity. Even hardened skeptics and high-ranking officials, upon meeting Him, would bow spontaneously; would-be debaters would find themselves speechless and humble in His presence. His enemies in the clergy warned curiosity-seekers to avoid Him lest they fall under His spell; they circulated absurd theories to account for His soul-stirring impact on credible witnesses. Bahá'u'lláh's character was as outstanding and unusual as His force of personality. His lifelong conduct was marked by courage, a passion for justice, self-sacrificing love for humanity, and airtight symmetry of word and deed.

Beyond such considerations as these, Bahá'u'lláh offers a subjective but highly intriguing proof of His divine mission: He claims – and millions of His followers believe – that His very words throb with spiritual power such as no human author can duplicate. He invites seekers to immerse themselves in the ocean of His words and, by seeking out the "hidden pearls" of meaning those words contain, to experience for themselves the creative and transforming influence of this power. This personal experiment enables any inquirer to evaluate, through the promptings of his or her own heart, whether Bahá'u'-lláh's writings are of divine or merely human origin. One can further test such a power by observing its apparent effects in the emergence of the Bahá'í worldwide community.

*****

These are some of the findings that, in my experience, seem to emerge from a systematic probing of Bahá'u'lláh's claim. No one needs to take my word for any of these statements. The evidence is open to any seeker who chooses to examine it. Let us suppose, therefore, that others repeat this investigation and verify these findings. In that case, how are we to explain them?

To me, the simplest, most elegant explanation is also the most obvious: Bahá'u'lláh's claim is true. He spoke and acted not of His own accord, but at the bidding of an all-encompassing Higher Power. This hypothesis neatly correlates and predicts everything we can discover about Bahá'u'lláh through empirical study. It is a scientific hypothesis in the strictest sense of the word; that is, any number of simple observations could conceivably remove it from serious consideration. Yet those observations, when performed, consistently have the opposite effect: Rather than rule it out, they fall into place in such a way as to strengthen our faith in the hypothesis.

Moreover, this explanation is, for me, the one that feels right. I try it on for size and find that somehow, in some way I cannot quite explain, it fits. It fits everything I can learn about Bahá'u'lláh, about myself, about other people, about life, religion, civilization, and whatnot. This intuitive "ring of truth" is not a strictly scientific consideration, although every true scientist uses it in evaluating scientific conclusions. It is a personal sense of rightness one cannot easily convey to others.

*****

Does this mean one can "prove" Bahá'u'lláh was Who He claimed to be? That depends. When I investigate the evidence for myself, I find it both satisfying and compelling. I therefore choose to act on it, confident that my decision to do so is rational and correct. Still, we may recognize that there are other ways to explain the facts about Bahá'u'lláh; other observers may prefer one of these alternative explanations.

A professor of the Moody Bible Institute, asked to comment on the Bahá'í Faith, replied: "There is no question about it. It is the work of the Devil." There we have an undeniably straightforward explanation which, with one bold stroke, covers all the facts – the successful prophecies, the scientific insights, the innate abilities, the uncanny attraction of Bahá'u'lláh's presence, and all the rest. I have not the first clue as to how one might disprove this hypothesis. My personal reason for rejecting it has to do with the words of Jesus Christ (Whose divine authority every Bahá'í accepts without reservation): "Ye shall know them by their fruits. Do men gather grapes of thorns, or figs of thistles?" (Matt. 7:16) Different readers interpret this touchstone in different ways; it may well have more than one correct interpretation. But whenever I try to apply it in any reasonable manner, it strengthens my confidence in the divine origin of Bahá'u'lláh's revelation. The overwhelmingly positive results, or "fruits," of His life and teachings speak for themselves.

We might attempt to explain Bahá'u'lláh as a time traveler from the distant future or as a space alien with telepathic powers. The former hypothesis would account for His scientific and prophetic knowledge; the latter might explain His extraordinary subjective impact on those who met Him. We could say He was a saintly superpsychic who – simply to perpetrate an elaborate hoax – willingly endured agonizing persecution and humiliation, a kind of living crucifixion lasting forty years. However amusing such ideas may seem, they remind us that there is no mathematically rigorous way to exclude even the most fanciful alternatives.

Any hypothesis intended to account for the qualities, accomplishments and motives of Bahá'u'lláh must also explain the appearance of similar signs in the Báb and 'Abdu'l-Bahá. The rapid and successive appearance of three closely linked figures with such unheard-of abilities is itself a phenomenon almost as remarkable as any single achievement by any one of them.

One may play endlessly with speculative theories designed to account for the facts surrounding the rise and establishment of the Bahá'í revelation. Most such theories, it seems to me, ignore at least some of the facts and still bog down in complexity. I know only one hypothesis that (1) explains all the facts in a simple, straightforward manner, (2) yields a variety of testable implications, and (3) survives every attempt to discredit it through observation and experience. That hypothesis is the one proposed earlier: Bahá'u'lláh really was a Manifestation of God.

Let Bahá'u'lláh state the case in His own words:

"Consider this wronged One. Though the clearest proofs attest the truth of His Cause; though the prophecies He, in an unmistakable language, hath made have been fulfilled; though, in spite of His not being accounted among the learned, His being unschooled and inexperienced in the disputations current among the divines, He hath rained upon men the showers of His manifold and Divinely-inspired knowledge; yet, behold how this generation hath rejected His authority, and rebelled against Him. . . . God grant that, with a penetrating vision and radiant heart, thou mayest observe the things that have come to pass and are now happening, and, pondering them in thine heart, mayest recognize that which most men have, in this Day, failed to perceive." (G 58)

*****

This book has set forth, to the best of my ability and understanding, the rational basis for my personal belief in Bahá'u'lláh. In writing it I have discussed a variety of subjects and presented a number of related arguments. Certain things, however, I have refrained from doing:

(1) I did not begin by attempting to demonstrate the existence of God through logical arguments. This does not mean I am writing only for those who already believe in God, nor does it mean I expect the reader necessarily to accept His existence as self-evident. It simply means I believe the strongest proof of God's reality is His periodic intervention in history through the founders of world religions – Moses, Christ, Buddha, Muḥammad, and all the others. Above all, it is the recurrence of His self-revelation in the person of Bahá'u'lláh, in this promised day of all ages. If we discover a broadcast coming over a radio, we need not precede our discussion of that discovery by proving logically the existence of a distant broadcaster. The voice of the broadcaster is proof enough. In a similar vein, Bahá'u'lláh says that "the gift of Divine Revelation . . . is God's supreme testimony, the clearest evidence of His truth." (ibid. 195)

(2) While discussing the fulfillment of prophecies contained in Bahá'í sacred texts, I have neglected a large category of related evidence: the fulfillment by Bahá'u'lláh Himself of prophecies from the Bible and other ancient scriptures. My reason for omitting this important topic is simply that it is treated fully in many other sources. Those wishing to pursue the matter are referred to such books as *Thief in the Night* by William Sears and *I Shall Come Again* by Hushidar Motlagh.

(3) I have not mentioned physical miracles. Every religion has its tales of supernatural healings and other wonderful acts purportedly performed by its founder; the Bahá'í Faith is no exception. Bahá'ís do not deny the reality of such happenings, for they believe God's Manifestations embody all His attributes – including divine omnipotence. Still, Bahá'ís are forbidden to offer such events as proofs of their religion's validity. Most "miracle" stories, even if true, are undocumented and anecdotal. Some refer to events that took place only in an inward or metaphorical sense. Even those that may have occurred literally are significant, as evidence, only to those who actually see them – and not always then. Accordingly, I have omitted any and all reports of inexplicable physical phenomena. Certain abilities cited as evidence by Bahá'u'lláh Himself, such as prophecy and rapid revelation-writing, may in some sense be regarded as miraculous; but that sense clearly is a non-physical one.

(4) I have not presumed to suggest what any reader should do about the conclusions offered here. Any person who, after investigation, accepts the claim of Bahá'u'lláh must of course decide how to integrate that insight into his or her life. Religious conviction has obvious and urgent implications for action. But such decisions are logically distinct from questions of truth or

falsity. The more determined one is to follow the facts wherever they lead, without regard to personal considerations, the more reliably one will be able to determine Bahá'u'lláh's real identity.

*****

That said, it remains my earnest conviction that incalculable benefits await anyone willing to investigate dispassionately the claim of Bahá'u'lláh and to follow through on the results of that investigation. If society collectively is not yet ready to reap those benefits, it will be ready in the none-too-distant future. Meanwhile, we as individuals can enjoy those benefits today. We can also hasten that future for the society in which we live. There is nothing to stop us.

"The Book of God is wide open," writes Bahá'u'lláh,

> *"and His Word is summoning mankind unto Him. No more than a mere handful, however, hath been found willing to cleave to His Cause, or to become the instruments for its promotion. These few have been endued with the Divine Elixir that can, alone, transmute into purest gold the dross of the world, and have been empowered to administer the infallible remedy for all the ills that afflict the children of men."* (ibid. 183)

> *"Take heed that ye do not vacillate in your determination to embrace the truth of this Cause – a Cause through which the potentialities of the might of God have been revealed, and His sovereignty established. With faces beaming with joy, hasten ye unto Him. . . . Through it the poor have been enriched, the learned enlightened, and the seekers enabled to ascend unto the presence of God. Beware, lest ye make it a cause of dissension amongst you. Be ye as firmly settled as the immovable mountain in the Cause of your Lord, the Mighty, the Loving."* (ibid. 136-7)

Appendix A
BECOMING A BAHÁ'Í

Bahá'ís are forbidden to proselytize or pressure others into accepting their beliefs. The only reason one should become a Bahá'í is because his or her heart has been touched by Bahá'u'lláh, the Glory of God. There can be no other valid reason.

Some respond quickly, others take longer, still others may never recognize Bahá'u'lláh's station at all. It is up to each individual to investigate the Cause of Bahá'u'lláh for himself or herself.

But if you can truthfully say . . .

❐ *I believe in Bahá'u'lláh as the Messenger of God for this age;*

❐ *I hereby affirm my wholehearted readiness to obey His laws and teachings; and*

❐ *I accept the authority of the institutions He has established;*

then you already are a Bahá'í in everything except name. We strongly encourage you, in that case, to "make it official" by registering as a member of the Bahá'í community. It is of course true that Bahá'í social, devotional and study activities are open to anyone, regardless of religious affiliation. Formal membership, however, carries exciting benefits. These include the right to vote in Bahá'í elections, hold Bahá'í administrative office, contribute to the Bahá'í Fund, and the like.

Your exact procedure will vary by locality. In many countries, such as the United States, new members typically fill out an enrollment card providing contact details and a signed declaration of faith. In others, an oral statement is sufficient. Any Bahá'í individual or institution in your area can assist you in taking this momentous step. If you are not in touch with them, and cannot find a local telephone listing for the Bahá'í Faith, then please go to *www.bahai.org* and click on "National Communities" (under the "Contact Information" heading). Then click on your own country for details.

pending on locality, your choices may include online enrollment via
ernet. In the United States, for instance, the web address for online
enrollment is *https://join.bahai.us/Invitation.aspx*.
All believers, new or old, are encouraged to learn as much as possible
about their Faith. While personal daily study of scripture is paramount,
Bahá'ís throughout the world also organize study circles to explore together
the teachings of Bahá'u'lláh, including various service practices through
which their community grows. We strongly encourage you to join this
lifelong process of learning.

For those with access to a computer or smart-phone, there are several
outstanding online resources:

One is the Bahá'í Reference Library: *http://reference.bahai.org/en/*. This
site provides electronic access to selected writings of the Bahá'í Faith in
English, Persian and Arabic. The home page defaults to English. To study
these writings in their original Persian or Arabic, click on the corresponding
option under "Languages".

Another terrific resource is the software program *Interfaith Explorer*,
ready for download from the web site *www.bahairesearch.com*. Available
for Windows (free), iPad (free), and the iPhone/iPod Touch ($1.99), this
program allows instant searching of 5,000 books in 22 languages. Included
are scriptures of all the great world religions – not only Bahá'í – as well as
regularly updated guidance from the Bahá'í Universal House of Justice.

Also highly recommended is *Heart to Heart* (*www.hearttoheartpublica
tions.com*), a slide show featuring approximately 700 important questions
about the Bahá'í Faith, answered with citations from relevant Bahá'í scriptures and authoritative texts. The pages are lavishly and beautifully illustrated
and logically sequenced under 18 topical headings – "Prayer and Medita-
tion", "Christ and Bahá'u'lláh", "Tests and Difficulties", and the like.

BIBLIOGRAPHY

MANY OLDER NON-BAHÁ'Í SOURCES cited in this volume are out of print. Some, however, are now online through the Google Books project. These include – possibly among others – the books listed here by Cheyne, Chirol, and Phelps. Anyone wishing to explore these originals as PDF scans can find them from the Google Books home page (*http://books.google.com*) by entering titles or authors into the search box. New works are added all the time, so it may be worthwhile to check back periodically.

(I was pleasantly surprised to find my own book, *The Challenge of Bahá'u'lláh*, online at Google Books in preview form. This means the reader can "thumb through" a few pages electronically. For copyright reasons, preview versions are neither intended nor practical for reading straight through. They differ in this respect from many older books for which copyright has expired and which one may therefore download or read online without restriction.)

As to Bahá'í sources: I have tried, in *The Case for Bahá'u'lláh*, to quote current editions of Bahá'í sacred texts and to identify those editions precisely in this bibliography. New editions, however, are always appearing. For any particular book, it is always possible that the version I used will differ in page numbering or other minor respects from the one available to a given reader.

One welcome antidote to such confusion is the online Bahá'i Reference Library (*http://reference.bahai.org*). This site provides electronic access to a comprehensive database of Baha'i authoritative texts in English, Persian, and Arabic. To locate the most current, "standard" source for any quoted passage, simply enter a fragment of its text into the search box. This will call up the complete passage, along with full context and up-to-date page and paragraph numbering.

'ABDU'L-BAHÁ. *'Abdu'l-Bahá in Canada.* Compiled by the National Spiritual Assembly of the Bahá'ís of Canada. Rev. ed. Thornhill, Ont.: Bahá'í Canada Publications, 1987.

———. *Memorials of the Faithful.* Translated from the Persian and annotated by Marzieh Gail. Wilmette, IL: Bahá'í Publishing Trust, 1997.

———. *Paris Talks: Addresses Given by 'Abdu'l-Bahá in 1911.* 12th ed. London: Bahá'í Publishing Trust, 1995.

———. *The Promulgation of Universal Peace: Talks Delivered by 'Abdu'l-Bahá during His Visit to the United States and Canada in 1912.* Compiled by Howard MacNutt. Wilmette, IL: Bahá'í Publishing Trust, 1982.

————. *The Secret of Divine Civilization.* Translated from the Persian by Marzieh
Gail in consultation with Ali-Kuli Khan. 1st pocket-size ed. Wilmette, IL:
Bahá'í Publishing Trust, 1990.

————. *Selections from the Writings of 'Abdu'l-Bahá.* Compiled by the Research
Department of the Universal House of Justice. Translated by a Committee
at the Bahá'í World Center and Marzieh Gail. 1st pocket-size ed. Wilmette,
IL: Bahá'í Publishing Trust, 1996.

————. *Some Answered Questions.* Compiled and translated by Laura Clifford Bar-
ney. 1st pocket-size ed. Wilmette, IL: Bahá'í Publishing Trust, 1984.

————. *Tablets of Abdul-Baha Abbas.* 3 vols. New York: Bahai Publishing Society, 1909-16.

————. *Tablets of the Divine Plan.* 1st pocket-size ed. Wilmette, IL: Bahá'í Publishing Trust, 1993.

————. *A Traveler's Narrative Written to Illustrate the Episode of the Báb.* Translated by Edward G. Browne. New and corrected ed. Wilmette, IL: Bahá'í
Publishing Trust, 1980.

————. *Will and Testament of 'Abdu'l-Bahá.* Wilmette, IL: Bahá'í Publishing
Trust, 1944.

Appreciations of the Bahá'í Faith. Wilmette, IL: Bahá'í Publishing Committee, 1947.

THE BÁB. *Selections from the Writings of the Báb.* Compiled by the Research Department of the Universal House of Justice. Translated by Habib
Taherzadeh et al. Haifa: Bahá'í World Centre, 1976.

BACH, MARCUS. *Strangers at the Door.* Nashville: Abingdon Press, 1971.

[BAHÁ'Í INTERNATIONAL COMMUNITY OFFICE OF PUBLIC INFORMATION.]
Bahá'u'lláh. Wilmette, IL: Bahá'í Publishing Trust, 1991.

BAHÁ'U'LLÁH. *Epistle to the Son of the Wolf.* Translated by Shoghi Effendi. 1st
pocket-size ed. Wilmette, IL: Bahá'í Publishing Trust, 1988.

————. *Gleanings from the Writings of Bahá'u'lláh.* Compiled and translated by
Shoghi Effendi. 1st pocket-size ed. Wilmette, IL: Bahá'í Publishing Trust,
1983.

————. *The Hidden Words.* Translated by Shoghi Effendi. Wilmette, IL: Bahá'í
Publishing, 2002.

————. *The Kitáb-i-Aqdas: The Most Holy Book.* 1st pocket-size ed. Wilmette, IL:
Bahá'í Publishing Trust, 1993.

————. *The Kitáb-i-Íqán: The Book of Certitude.* Translated by Shoghi Effendi.
Wilmette, IL: Bahá'í Publishing, 2003.

————. *Prayers and Meditations.* Translated from the original Persian and Arabic
by Shoghi Effendi. 1st pocket-size ed. Wilmette, IL: Bahá'í Publishing
Trust, 1987.

————. *The Seven Valleys and The Four Valleys.* Translated by Marzieh Gail with
Ali-Kuli Khan. Wilmette, IL: Bahá'í Publishing Trust, 1991.

————. *The Summons of the Lord of Hosts: Tablets of Bahá'u'lláh.* Haifa: Bahá'í
World Centre, 2002.

————. *Tablets of Bahá'u'lláh revealed after the Kitáb-i-Aqdas.* Compiled by the
Research Department of the Universal House of Justice. Translated by

Habib Taherzadeh et. al. 1st pocket-size ed. Wilmette, IL: Bahá'í Publishing Trust, 1988.

BAHÁ'U'LLÁH AND 'ABDU'L-BAHÁ. *Bahá'í World Faith: Selected Writings of Bahá'u'lláh and 'Abdu'l-Bahá.* Wilmette, IL: Bahá'í Publishing Trust, 1976.

BALYUZI, H. M. *'Abdu'l-Bahá: The Centre of the Covenant of Bahá'u'lláh.* London: George Ronald, 1971.

―――. *The Báb: The Herald of the Day of Days.* Oxford: George Ronald, 1973.

―――. *Bahá'u'lláh: The King of Glory.* Oxford: George Ronald, 1980.

BLOMFIELD, LADY (SITÁRIH KHÁNUM). *The Chosen Highway.* Wilmette, IL: Bahá'í Publishing Trust, n.d.; repr. 1975.

CHEYNE, T. K. *The Reconciliation of Races and Religions.* London: Adam and Charles Black, 1914.

CHIROL, SIR VALENTINE. *The Middle Eastern Question or Some Political Problems of Indian Defence.* London: John Murray, 1903.

CLARK, RONALD W. *Einstein – The Life and Times.* New York: Avon Books, 1972.

CLARKE, ARTHUR C. *Profiles of the Future.* London: Victor Gollancz Ltd., 1982.

COOPER, L. *An Introduction to the Meaning and Structure of Physics.* New York: Harper & Row, 1968.

COTRAN, RAMZI S., VINAY KUMAR, AND STANLEY L. ROBBINS. *Robbins Pathologic Basis of Disease.* Philadelphia: W. B. Saunders: 1989.

DULBECCO, RENATO, AND HAROLD S. GINSBERG. *Virology.* Philadelphia: J. B. Lippincott, 1988.

ESSLEMONT, J. E. *Bahá'u'lláh and the New Era: An Introduction to the Bahá'í Faith.* 5th rev. ed. Wilmette, IL: Bahá'í Publishing Trust, 1980.

Establishing World Peace. Compiled by the Research Department of the Universal House of Justice. Haifa: Bahá'í World Centre, 1985.

FERRIS, TIMOTHY. *Coming of Age in the Milky Way.* New York: Anchor Books, 1980.

GAIL, MARZIEH. *Summon Up Remembrance.* Oxford: George Ronald, 1987.

GARDNER, MARTIN. *Relativity for the Million.* New York: MacMillan, 1962.

GAMOW, GEORGE. *The Birth and Death of the Sun.* New York: Viking Press, 1946.

GIACHERY, UGO. "One God, One Truth, One People." *The Bahá'í World: An International Record, Volume XV, 1967-1973.* Compiled by the Universal House of Justice. Haifa: Bahá'í World Centre, 1975.

GOBINEAU, JOSEPH ARTHUR LE COMTE DE. *Les Religions et les Philosophies dans l'Asie Centrale.* Paris: Les Éditions G. Crés et Cie., 1928.

HATCHER, WILLIAM S. AND J. DOUGLAS MARTIN. *The Bahá'í Faith: The Emerging Global Religion.* Wilmette, IL: Bahá'í Publishing, 2002.

HAWKING, STEPHEN W. *A Brief History of Time.* New York: Bantam Books, 1988.

HOFMAN, DAVID. *Bahá'u'lláh, The Prince of Peace: A Portrait.* Oxford: George Ronald, 1992.

HONNOLD, ANNAMARIE. *Vignettes from the Life of 'Abdu'l-Bahá.* Oxford: George Ronald, 1992.

121

JORDAN, DANIEL C. *Becoming Your True Self.* Wilmette, IL: Bahá'í Publishing Trust, 1968.

LEDERMAN, LEON, AND DICK TERESI. *The God Particle.* New York: Dell, 1993.

Lights of Guidance: A Bahá'í Reference File. Compiled by Helen Hornby. New Delhi: Bahá'í Publishing Trust, 1988.

LOVEJOY, C. OWEN. "Evolution of Human Walking." *Scientific American* (November 1988): 89.

MARCELLA, ELENA MARIA. *The Quest for Eden.* New York: Philosophical Library, 1966.

MATTHEWS, GARY L. *The Challenge of Bahá'u'lláh.* Oxford: George Ronald, 1999.

———. *He Cometh with Clouds: A Bahá'í View of Christ's Return.* Oxford: George Ronald, 1996.

MISNER, CHARLES W., KIP S. THORNE, AND JOHN A. WHEELER. *Gravitation.* San Francisco: Freeman, 1973.

MOTLAGH, HUSHIDAR. *I Shall Come Again.* Mt. Pleasant, MI: Global Perspectives, 1992.

NABÍL-I-A'ZAM (MUHAMMAD-I-ZARANDÍ). *The Dawn-Breakers: Nabíl's Narrative of the Early Days of the Bahá'í Revelation.* Translated from the original Persian and edited by Shoghi Effendi. Wilmette, IL: Bahá'í Publishing Trust, 1932.

[NATIONAL SPIRITUAL ASSEMBLY OF THE BAHÁ'ÍS OF JAPAN, comp.]. *Japan Will Turn Ablaze! Tablets of 'Abdu'l-Bahá, Letters of Shoghi Effendi And Historical Notes About Japan.* Japan: Bahá'í Publishing Trust, 1974.

NICOLAS, A.L.M. *Siyyid 'Alí-Muhammad dit le Báb.* Paris: Librairie Critique, 1908.

PHELPS, MYRON. *Life and Teachings of 'Abbás Effendi.* New York: Knickerbocker Press, 1912.

RABBANI, RÚHÍYYIH. *The Desire of the World: Materials for the contemplation of God and His Manifestation for this Day.* Oxford: George Ronald, 1961.

ROBBINS, STANLEY, AND VINAY KUMAR. *Basic Pathology.* Philadelphia: W. B. Saunders, 1987.

SEARS, WILLIAM. *Thief in the Night: Or The Strange Case of the Missing Millennium.* Oxford: George Ronald, 1961.

SHOGHI EFFENDI. *The Advent of Divine Justice.* 1st pocket-size ed. Wilmette, IL: Bahá'í Publishing Trust, 1990.

———. *Bahá'í Administration: Selected Messages 1922-1932.* 7th ed. Wilmette, IL: Bahá'í Publishing Trust, 1974.

———. *Citadel of Faith: Messages to America, 1947-1957.* Wilmette, IL: Bahá'í Publishing Trust, 1965.

———. *Dawn of a New Day.* New Delhi: Bahá'í Publishing Trust, [1970].

———. *God Passes By.* Wilmette, IL: Bahá'í Publishing Trust, 1944.

———. *High Endeavours: Messages to Alaska.* Compiled by the National Spiritual Assembly of the Bahá'ís of Alaska. N.p.: National Spiritual Assembly of the Bahá'ís of Alaska, 1976.

[———]. *Letters from the Guardian to Australia and New Zealand, 1923-1957.* [Australia]: National Spiritual Assembly of the Bahá'ís of Australia, 1970.

————. *Messages to the Bahá'í World, 1950-1957.* Rev. ed. Wilmette, IL: Bahá'í Publishing Trust, 1971.

————. *Messages to Canada.* N.p.: National Spiritual Assembly of the Bahá'ís of Canada, 1965.

————. *Principles of Bahá'í Administration: A Compilation.* 3d ed. London: Bahá'í Publishing Trust, 1973.

————. *The Promised Day Is Come.* 1st pocket-size ed. Wilmette, IL: Bahá'í Publishing Trust, 1996.

————. *Selected Writings of Shoghi Effendi.* Compiled by the Bahá'í Publishing Committee. 2d ed. Wilmette, IL: Bahá'í Publishing Trust, 1975.

————. *This Decisive Hour: Messages from Shoghi Effendi to the North American Bahá'ís, 1932-1946.* Wilmette, IL: Bahá'í Publishing Trust, 2002.

————. *The Unfolding Destiny of the British Bahá'í Community: The Messages of the Guardian of the Bahá'í Faith to the Bahá'ís of the British Isles.* London: Bahá'í Publishing Trust, 1981.

————. *The World Order of Bahá'u'lláh: Selected Letters.* 1st pocket-size ed. Wilmette, IL: Bahá'í Publishing Trust, 1991.

————, comp. *The Bahá'í Faith 1844-1952.* Wilmette, IL: Bahá'í Publishing Committee, 1953.

Synopsis and Codification of the Laws and Ordinances of the Kitáb-i-Aqdas. Haifa, Israel: The Universal House of Justice, 1973.

TAHERZADEH, ADIB. *The Revelation of Bahá'u'lláh: Baghdád, 1853-63.* Volume 1. Oxford: George Ronald, 1974.

————. *The Revelation of Bahá'u'lláh: Adrianople, 1863-68.* Volume 2. Oxford: George Ronald, 1977.

————. *The Revelation of Bahá'u'lláh: 'Akká, 1868-77.* Volume 3. Oxford: George Ronald, 1983.

————. *The Revelation of Bahá'u'lláh: Mazra'ih & Bahjí, 1877-92.* Volume 4. Oxford: George Ronald, 1987.

THOMPSON, JULIET. *The Diary of Juliet Thompson.* Los Angeles: Kalimát Press, 1983.

TOYNBEE, ARNOLD. *A Study of History, vol. VIII.* London: Oxford University Press, 1954.

UNIVERSAL HOUSE OF JUSTICE. *The Constitution of the Universal House of Justice.* Haifa: Bahá'í World Centre, 1972.

————. *Individual Rights and Freedoms in the World Order of Bahá'u'lláh.* Wilmette, IL: Bahá'í Publishing Trust, 1989.

————. *Messages from the Universal House of Justice, 1963-1986: The Third Epoch of the Formative Age.* Compiled by Geoffry W. Marks. Wilmette, IL: Bahá'í Publishing Trust, 1996.

WILBUR, KEN, ED. *Quantum Questions: Mystical Writings of the World's Great Physicists.* Boulder: Shambhala, 1984.

WOLF, FRED ALAN. *Taking the Quantum Leap.* New York: Perennial Library, 1989.

YOUNGHUSBAND, SIR FRANCIS. *The Gleam.* London: John Murray, 1923.

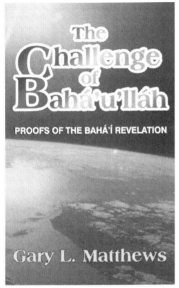

THE CASE FOR BAHÁ'U'LLÁH

THE CASE FOR BAHÁ'U'LLÁH

Made in the USA
Columbia, SC
08 October 2024

43929507R00072